101 Things to Do on Lake Minnetonka

101 Things to Do on Lake Minnetonka

Chris Dinesen Rogers

Dedication

My favorite Lake Minnetonka story happened during Thanksgiving weekend 2004. My mother came to visit us for the first time, along with my oldest sister. It was a cold and dreary November, with a dusting of snow swirling on the frozen ground. Everything took on the dull, brown color that marks the end of summer and the promise of the cold winter.

Nevertheless, my mother seated herself at the head of our kitchen table opposite the picture window with a view that looked out over the lake. For every meal I prepared and every spare moment we had, she would sit there just staring at the lake. She told me she could sit there all day because she couldn't get enough of the view. It's been several years since she passed, but I will never forget the joy in her face as she sat looking at that lake view. It is to her that I dedicate this book.

Thanks, Mom

Contents

Acknowledgments

The author acknowledges the following:

- Lake Minnetonka image: © OpenStreetMap contributors, http://www.openstreetmap.org/copyright
- Cover Image, Credit/Copyright Attribution: Michael Coddington/Shutterstock

Introduction

Lake Minnetonka formed about 11,000 years ago with the deposition of an end-moraine by the Wisconsin Glacial Episode, which occurred between 85,000 to 11,000 years ago. Geologically speaking, it is relatively young. But its 11,000 year lifespan has been nothing short of a wild ride.

It has seen ownership by three nations: France, Spain, France again, and finally, the United States. In its early days, six different territories claimed the lake after the United States acquired it with the Louisiana Purchase in 1803. Its history includes stints as part of the Louisiana, Missouri, Michigan, Wisconsin, and Iowa territories, before becoming a part of the Minnesota territory in 1849.

The story of Lake Minnetonka's discovery by white settlers begins in 1822. Prior to this time, its existence was virtually unknown to white settlers. Remember that the Lake Minnetonka area differed greatly from what it is today. The Big Woods stood intact. It provided a formidable barrier to anyone exploring west of the Mississippi River.

Then, there were the wetlands and marshes, along with the mosquitoes that come with them. And, the times were different. Relations between the Dakota and the settlers wouldn't have provided an incentive for exploration.

Joseph Brown and John Snelling, both at Fort Snelling, took a trip into Indian country. Following Minnehaha Creek, they found the lake. However, some accounts give that credit to Eli Pettijohn and Willis Moffett, which the evidence supports. Governor Alexander Ramsey christened the lake in 1852.

And it all began with a secret. Protected by the Big Woods, white settlers didn't know it existed. But once the secret got out, Lake Minnetonka became what some referred to as the *Saratoga of the West*, in a nod to Saratoga Springs, a popular tourist destination in New York.

The lives of the lake and its people changed forever with the Sioux (Dakota) Treaty of 1851. Settlers established Minnetonka Mills the following year at Minnehaha Creek downstream from Grays Bay. Establishment of Excelsior in 1853 and Wayzata in 1854 set the stage for the flood of settlers and tourists that would follow.

Settlement of Lake Minnetonka exploded. The Preemption Act allowed claims of 160 acres of eligible federal land. The land rush was on. It was a tumultuous period of land grabs and claim jumpers. Three townships encompassed Lake Minnetonka: Excelsior, Minnetonka, and Minnetrista. By the time the dust settled, settlers had claimed the entire lake shore by 1855, though some sources list 1859.

The Lake Minnetonka area has experienced several definitive periods in its existence after white settler claimed its shores. From its Glory Years of hotels and boarding houses to it Golden Age of streetcar boats and the Big Island Amusement Park to its Modern Era of lake residents, the lake has seen everything.

Lake Minnetonka became a destination for tourists and sportsmen, for the adventurous and the unwell. It attracted the elite and the *Empire Builder*, the shipbuilders and pioneers. Today, the lake lures visitors like you to its beautiful waters and stunning scenery. It's so many things, for so many people.

It is a northern pike striking hard on a lure. It is the plaintive cry of the loon, bouncing off the water's surface and wandering through the trees. It is the swish-swish sound of skis cutting a path through newly-fallen snow. It is clouds of mosquitoes and schools of sunnies. Lake Minnetonka is all you expect it to be and everything you do not. It is the big water. It is Lake Minnetonka.

How to Use This Book

I'm giving you the road map or passport, if you will; you're writing the story. And with Lake Minnetonka the story is as diverse as its people and history. In my previous travel book, *101 Things to Do on the Wisconsin Great River Road*, my readers often commented that they had business owners sign their book to verify they had visited a place. It's something for you to consider for making your journey your own.

The order of villages is presented as a scenic route going around the lake. It's worth mentioning that many places around Lake Minnetonka are private, including those which exist where the cool points of interest used to be found. Please, respect the privacy of residents, including parking restrictions and private roads. To the locals, it's not a landmark; it's their home.

For some sites that are not accessible by land, you can still view many of them from the water. Look for the sites designated as best by water. And remember that life doesn't stand still, even on Lake Minnetonka. Be sure to check events and businesses before planning your trip.

A Note to the Reader and Traveler: Every attempt was made to verify the information in this book to add to your enjoyment of Lake Minnetonka. But as with memories, time has a way of altering the stories and the tales. Even what would appear to be concrete facts depends upon the source. For example, I found the acreage of the lake varied widely, but I settled on the DNR's numbers. The author regrets any misinformation that has made it into this volume and any omissions. Visit by my website, chrisdinesenrogers.com, and drop me a line.

On a side note, I focused primarily on sites within the immediate vicinity of Lake Minnetonka, including other areas that figured prominently in its history. Omissions of other attractions and sites beyond this scope is in keeping in line with this goal.

Map of Lake Minnetonka

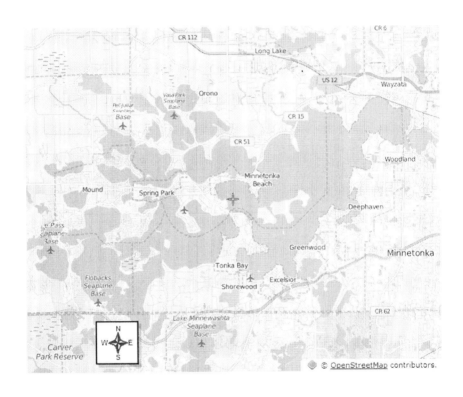

PART I

Wayzata

Wayzata became the gateway to Lake Minnetonka after its founding in 1853. But it took the railroad to put it on the map. Before 1868, Long Lake was *the* destination spot west of St. Anthony, aka, Minneapolis. The town had several businesses, including a sawmill and barrel factory. Once the railroad came to Wayzata, the village changed forever.

Its history became linked with the railroad and the legendary *Empire Builder*, James J. Hill. What naysayers referred to as *"Hill's Folly"* was both a boon and a curse to the town. The railroad brought tourists and revenue to the area. It ushered in Wayzata's hotel history.

However, the railroad also threatened the town's existence. The infamous feud between the village of Wayzata and James Hill erupted, fueled by flagging tourism and the relocation of the train depot. Wayzata struggled.

With the reconciliation between Wayzata and Hill, its threatened demise was averted. It was no longer the "*little train stop on your way to Long Lake*." Instead, the village flourished. Today, Wayzata has embraced its past and its struggles. And it continues its reign as one of the premier spots to enjoy Lake Minnetonka.

Join in the Fun at James Hill Days

In the tradition of James Hill himself, Wayzata's James J. Hill Days (JJHD) honoring the late railroad magnate is a must-see. There's something for everyone with the slew of events on tap for the weekend bash. Whether you want to shop at the market or dance the night away, you'll find plenty to do for everyone in the family. The Lake Minnetonka Carnival will keep the kids happy, while Mom and Dad might enjoy sampling craft beers at the Rails & Ales Beer Festival.

Everyone will enjoy rooting for their favorite hound at the Dachshund Races. Scouts in the family can show off their racing skills at the Coaster Cart Derby. If classic cars are more your speed, be sure and take in the Motorsports Show. And your day wouldn't be complete if you didn't try your hand at finding the gold spike. You can pick up daily clues starting the Tuesday before the event. And new for 2016, the First Annual JJHD Wakesurf Throwdown.

Did You Know? The first celebration honoring James Hill and his Great Northern Railroad to the Pacific Coast was in St. Paul in 1883.

Wayzata Chamber of Commerce
402 East Lake Street Wayzata
952-473-9595
info@wayzatachamber.com
jamesjhilldays.com

***

James J. Hill's Legacy

"Most men who have really lived have had, in some share, their great adventure. This railway is mine."

If there is one name linked with Wayzata, it is James J. Hill, aka, the Empire Builder. It was his vision that brought the railroad to Wayzata and opened the Lake Minnetonka area to the rest of the world. His story is one of survival and tenacity. Born on September 16, 1838 in Ontario, Hill came from a poor family. Despite these obstacles, he persevered to create his own company and history. His break into the industry started ironically enough with the Panic of 1873. This financial crisis in both North America and Europe would last until 1879.

Hill bought the St. Paul and Pacific Railroad that later became the St. Paul, Minneapolis, and Manitoba Railway and later still, the Great Northern. Under his leadership, the railroad reached Puget Sound by 1893. It wasn't just the railroad, but also the economic development and settlement of immigrants along the way that changed the region. He encouraged settlement along the line, creating an economic boon. But James Hill's relationship with Wayzata had its rough times too.

Conflict was perhaps inevitable with the railroad near the shoreline. It began with a lawsuit against E.B. Sanders who built a lake house in what Hill perceived as the path of the railroad. The village did not sit on the sidelines, watching the events unfold idly, Instead, they in turn, made the issue a village matter with a counter suit. The village of Wayzata won, giving it the right-of-way to the water's edge at both Walker Street and Broadway. But the victory wouldn't last.

Hill himself countered by moving the depot a mile to the east in Holdridge in 1893, essentially putting Wayzata out of the picture. He reportedly said, "*Let them walk a mile for the next twenty years.*" Finally, the feud ended in 1905.

In a magnanimous gesture, Hill had the present-day depot built, calling it the most beautiful one on his line. And with James J. Hill Days, this chapter of conflict and lawsuits has been closed.

James Hill moved on to take up other business ventures. He passed on the business to his son in 1907. He continued to work until the week before he died. On May 29, 1916, James J. Hill passed away in his St. Paul home. As a tribute to Hill, all traffic on Hill's roads and all boats on the Hill's lines stopped for five minutes, from 2 p.m. to 2:05 p.m., on May 30, 1916.

"Give me Swedes, snuff, and whiskey, and I'll build a railroad through hell."

2

Step Back in Time at One of the First Lake Hotels

Stand at the corner of Lake Street and Broadway Avenue. Imagine gazing out your window over the bay. Forget the noise from the railroads and steamers; the view still captivated you. This is the scene that lured visitors to Lake Minnetonka, setting the stage for the era of hotels and tourism.

While Wayzata wasn't a destination like Excelsior, it boasted several hotels and boarding houses in its early days. One of the first hotels, the Maurer House, stood at the intersection of Lake Street and Broadway Avenue.

Patrons loved the hotel's billiard hall, along with its well-stocked bar and cigars. It even had its own dock. Captain O.L. West, steamboat pilot of the *Belle of Minnetonka*, took over the hotel in 1889, renaming it the West Hotel. It lasted for about 10 years. before it was torn down in 1900.

Corner of Lake Street and Broadway Avenue, Wayzata

***

Wayzata Hotel History

Wayzata's foray into the hotel business was short and not quite as large compared to other towns around Lake Minnetonka. One could blame the railroad. Sure, it brought the tourists into town. But, in the early days, the trains were loud, dirty, and foul-smelling. Staying down wind of the barrage of smoke given off from the locomotives wouldn't be a draw. The steamboats spewing their black smoke also added to the unpleasantness. But, it might even be simpler than that.

Imagine riding into town after a tiring journey. You step off the train and look out over Wayzata Bay. You are awestruck. Maybe you see steamers in the distance. You feel the cool breeze off the lake. What do you want to do? Experience the lake! Perhaps it was the lake itself that lured visitors away from Wayzata, making them eager to explore this marvelous place.

Wayzata's hotels began with the early settlers. After a difficult journey, a room at a boarding house or hotel was welcome. One of the early settlers, John Stevens Harrington, built a cabin in 1854 in what is now Ferndale in the south section of Wayzata. He later added 16 rooms and changed its name to the Harrington Inn, the first summer hotel on the lake. And so began the hotel era.

In the early days, the overcrowded hotels were in high demand. Residents often took in travelers. These impressions must have made a lasting impact. A later advertisement for the Old Orchard in Excelsior left no doubt about its terms. *"Not over sixty guests can be taken care of at Old Orchard without crowding."*

Hotels also changed owners, often multiple times. The Maurer House, for example, became the Minnetonka Hotel, which became the West Hotel. A few others popped up in the later 1880s, including the Dudley's Hotel, Abel Day's Hotel, and B.F. Keesling's place. But the grandest of them all opened its doors in 1880.

The Arlington House was the largest of Wayzata's hotels, with over 100 rooms, especially popular with southern guests. The three-story building overlooked Wayzata Bay, providing stunning views of the lake. Looking out over Wayzata Bay from downtown, the Arlington House once stood on the rise to your left.

The end of the Arlington House might leave you shaking your head. James Hill wanted to clear the way for the Hotel Lafayette's success. Hill wanted his hotel to be the grandest and most successful place on the lake. He'd make sure that nothing stood in its way.

So, Hill rented the entire Arlington House. It never opened again. A fire put the languishing hotel out of its misery in 1890. It was the end of an era for Wayzata's hotels. The village would suffer with the loss of tourist revenue with the Arlington House's demise.

While the Arlington House was the last of the large hotels, smaller businesses still existed. The Northland Inn opened in 1901 north of LaSalle Avenue near Highway 101 on the first train stop after Minneapolis. It provided year-round accommodations for 50 guests, something that stood out among the many seasonal establishments. It featured electric lights and a parlor with view overlooking the lake.

To keep the business solvent the entire year, it had to attract guests after the busy summer season. Taking a lesson from the Mound hotels, the manager reached out to anglers and sportsmen with special events. The hotel stayed in business until it closed in 1915. New owners converted into an apartment building. Only one hotel stayed open well into the 20th century, the Gleason House.

The Gleason House stood at the corner of Lake Street and Walker Avenue. Travelers knew it as an affordable place to stay, charging $14 a week, including meals. In today's money, you'd pay about $280 a week, a heck of a deal by today's standards—especially if the food was good!

Unlike other hotels around the lake, the Gleason House was one of the few to keep the same name through the years. Most went through multiple name changes with successive owners. Built in 1871, it outlasted them all until it too closed in 1964.

Abel's Day Inn (1854-?)
Arlington House (1880-1890)
B.F. Keesling's Hotel (1856-1858)
Dudley's Hotel (1855-1861)
Gleason House (1871-1964)
Harrington Inn (1854-1899)
Maurer House (1870-1900)
Newark Hotel (1857-1892)
Northland Inn (1901-1915)

3

Make it a Day at the Wayzata Beach

A day on Lake Minnetonka wouldn't be complete without a day at the beach. And the Wayzata Beach has lots to offer for a day of fun and sun. Whether you want to swim or fish, the beach has you covered. Come by land or boat to enjoy its garden and summer concessions. There's even an outdoor shower to wash off all the sand between your toes. Want to get on the water? Rent a kayak or a canoe.

Looking for a more relaxing time? Find yourself one of the beach's Adirondack chairs and take in the cool and refreshing lake breezes. There's a reason, after all, why Wayzata got its name, which means Northern god of the north who blows cold wind.

Note: Public parking is available in the municipal-owned lot. But, the closest spots are reserved for permitted parking. Sorry, only available for city residents.

Located across the walking bridge from Shaver Park
Docking available at the short-term public boat docks
Information: 952-404-5300

***

Snapshot of the 1850s

- 1852: Treaty of Traverse des Sioux

- 1852: Lake Minnetonka named by Governor Ramsey

- 1852: Excelsior Pioneer Association established

- 1852: First Lake Minnetonka settlement in what was then called Minnetonka Mills

- 1852: Hennepin County organized

- 1853: Dam at Minnetonka Mills completed

- 1854: Wayzata laid out

- 1854: Cook's House opens in Mound City

- 1854: Excelsior Post Office officially established

- 1854: First store in Excelsior opened at corner of Second and Center Streets

- 1854: Excelsior's first schoolhouse opened

- 1855: Excelsior Commons created

- 1855: Wayzata's first postal service

- 1855: First squatters received good titles for the lands they entered at the US Land Office

- 1855: First stagecoach from St. Anthony to Wayzata

- 1855: *Song of Hiawatha* published by Henry Wadsworth Longfellow
- 1856-1858: The grasshopper plague devastated the area
- 1857-1861: Ginseng era
- 1858: Minnesota became the 32nd state
- 1858: Wayzata's first schoolhouse opened

4

Learn the Story of Spirit Knob

Looking out from Wayzata Bay, you'll notice two distinct features. To your left is a strip of land that juts out into the bay, known as Breezy Point. Spirit Knob, also known as Point Wakon or Place of Spirits, was a point on the end that extended farther into the bay. Another account refers to it as Wa-na-gee Pa-ze-dan-Spirit Knob or little hill of the spirit.

When it existed, Spirit Knob was a prominent feature you could not miss. The legend said that the Dakota Indians considered it a sacred place where they put scalps on a rock and built fires for ceremonies. Early photographs of Wayzata Bay often show the prominent point. Spirit Knob stood about 50 foot tall with a lone tree on its crest, giving it a Joshua Tree kind-of-feel.

Another legend refers to the spirit of a Dakota mother, who lost her only child to the lake during a storm. She would wail at midnight, lamenting her loss. Taken along with Wayzata's naming referring to the Northern god blowing cold wind, it's not surprising that the residents experienced an eerie feeling about it.

If you look to the right of the point, you'll see a small island, known as Spirit Island. Like Spirit Knob, the island held a similar place of honor for the Dakota to protect the north shore to Spirit Knob's south shore.

A stereograph image of Spirit Knob exists in the National Anthropological Archives, Smithsonian collection of George V. Allen. Allen was an attorney from Kansas and an early member of the National Stereoscope Association. The stereograph is one of many photographs in his collection of American Indians and the American frontier, circa 1860-1935. The collection includes several items, including mounted prints, autochromes, and glass negatives, documenting images of the American West with American Indian and frontier themes.

Note: This location is best viewed by water, though you can see Breezy Point from the shore. The point is privately owned.

Breezy Point, Wayzata Bay

***

What Happened to the Knob?

As you can see, Spirit Knob no longer exists. This is where its story gets interesting. Speculation remains about what happened afterward. One account says that it was brought to St. Paul by a mysterious Dr. S. from St. Louis and taken back home to a St. Louis museum.

Others look toward John Stevens Harrington, of Wayzata fame. The story goes that Harrington dug out the knob. Then, it was transported to Pittsburgh and then Washington, D.C. The knob, it was said, was a *"relic of barbarous days"* that settlers would assume forget. Harrington later confirmed this version of events in an 1887 interview in the *Northwestern Tourist*.

But yet another account said that a storm washed away Spirit Knob by 1880. The members of the Breezy Point Club bought the point in 1879. The club consisted of six men who purchased the land on which they later built a clubhouse. But as the name may suggest, the Breezy Point Club was a club for men; women not allowed. Allegedly, one condition of the club was that members had to stay single.

Perhaps the best explanation comes from Ellen Wilson Meyer's, *Tales of Tonka*. Author, Elizabeth Fries Ellet visited the Lake Minnetonka area in 1852. She reported in her book, *Summer Rambles in the West*, about a Dr. S from St. Louis. She wrote that he had brought the stone to St. Paul in 1852.

Another report seems to corroborate this story. Colonel John P. Owens wrote in the September 11, 1852 edition of the *Weekly Minnesotan* that *"until a month or six weeks ago,"* Spirit Knob had been in place. Later when Breezy Point Club acquired the knob, they said that the stone was gone. However, other evidence of the Dakota remained. In fact, the Breezy Point Club tried to save the knob. But Nature was determined to have Her way, eroding any remnants.

If anything remained of Spirit Knob, the club wiped out any traces in 1884 by leveling the area. And neither the Breezy Point Club nor Spirit Knob still exist today. To this day, no one knows what became of Spirit Knob.

Fishing Tip: Word around the campfire is that Breezy Point is a good place to land a smallmouth bass.

5

Making History

The site of the present-day Cov Restaurant on East Lake Street occupies a space with a long history of importance to the Wayzata. One of its greatest claims to fame is its place at the site of the first public Fourth of July celebration in 1855. So, began its long legacy of local importance.

The site started as a saloon owned by George Reid. Alas, Reid's tavern didn't last long after the Drys won the vote. (See Excelsior Brew Tour.) Reid's saloon then became one of the beloved sites of the past, the Lamb Bros Dry Goods Store in 1906. The store advertised "*Staple and fancy groceries, notions, fresh vegetables and fruits in season, drugs, dry good, and shoes.*" Surely, this list covered most needs.

When Lamb Bros Dry Goods Store closed in 1927, the Harts Cafe took over the site after extensive renovations to the building. The cafe too was a much-loved place, dare I say, iconic establishment, staying in business until 1983 when it too closed.

The rest of the story is familiar to locals. After the Harts Cafe closed its doors, the Sunset Restaurant took over the site. And after it served its final martini, the Cov Restaurant opened. While you're here, have a cocktail at the Cov Restaurant and raise a glass to history.

Cov Restaurant
700 East Lake Street, Wayzata
952-473-5253
covwayzata.com

***

The Loch Long Monster?

If you were around during the summer of 1912, you might have something to worry about. Rumors starting flying about a so-called sea serpent in nearby Long Lake. First, there was a sighting. Then, a shot rang out when it opened its large mouth, barring its teeth. More alleged sightings followed, attracting crowds and reporters. This all went on for three weeks.

But if this sounds fishy, rest assured the truth was soon exposed. Sam Rettinger, Long Lake's first funeral director and Ford Model T salesman, had carried out the hoax. Old timers will remember the Rettinger Motor Company on Lake Street in Wayzata, which he built in 1927.

The story goes that one of his co-conspirators ratted him out when the riggings of ropes and pulleys for the constructed serpent became too heavy, prompting him to walk off the job. Then, a couple kids rowed out and retrieved the 20-foot wood and muslin-covered "monster." Why the ruse, you ask? Word around the campfire is that Rettinger planned the hoax while his wife traveled. Can't leave these boys alone for a minute!

However, it wasn't the first time that reports of a serpent surfaced around the lake. In April 1887, workers on the Grays Bay Bridge reported seeing a mysterious serpent on the water for several minutes before it plunged back into the water and vanished from sight. Those sea serpents really got around—or at least one of those muskies.

6

See Grays Bay and Walk the Dam Trail

To get the full experience, walk the boardwalk trail from the Grays Bay Dam. Once on the trail, turn to look back at Minnehaha Creek. This view of the surrounding wetlands gives you a feel for what the area was like when the settlers first made their way here. Then, turn toward the lake.

Forget the houses and other modern-day trappings. Picture the mouth of Lake Minnetonka and the surrounding area as the settlers first encountered it. Impressive, huh? The wetlands provide an ideal setting for viewing wildlife and birdwatching. It also makes for good habitat for frogs and toads too.

Be sure to pack your binoculars—and mosquito repellent. This is Minnesota after all. An often-quoted letter from 1852 gives a dire account of the ravages of the mosquitoes. Early settler, Hezekiah Brake, received a panicked letter from his mother back in England.

Her letter warned him of traveling in this part of the country because he would "... *have your precious blood sucked out of you by mosquitoes—for a woman here told me they have trunks like elephants...*" I don't know about the elephant part, but the rest sounds accurate.

Did You Know? Author, Elizabeth Fries Ellet of New York, named Grays Bay Lake Browning in honor of poet, Elizabeth Barrett Browning when she visited the area in 1852. Her book, *Summer Rambles in the West*, describes her trip to Lake Minnetonka and other travels.

***

Grays Bay

Established in 1967, the Minnehaha Creek Watershed District (MCWD) monitors lake levels and the flow of Minnehaha Creek and the Minnehaha Creek Watershed. Grays Bay Dam is managed to reduce flooding both on the lake and downstream on the creek. The district keeps tabs on dry periods to support the health of the stream and safeguard wildlife and its habitat. Grays Bay Dam as you see it now was built in 1979.

Before that time, a wooden weir had controlled water flow since 1897. In 1897, the decision was made to build the dam which would forever change Minnehaha Creek, making it navigable only by canoe. The county condemned the land. At that time, the area resembled Old Channel Bay. Today, the MCWD monitors the lake with the control level at 929.4 feet above sea level. Changes to it, up or down, affect how it's managed.

To get to the dam site, follow Gray's Bay Blvd from the Gray's Bay boat launch. The road snakes through a residential area. Be sure and stay on the boulevard. There is limited free parking at the site. A number of informational signs give a good overview.

Did You Know? One-third of all boat launches at public access sites happen at Grays Bay.

Minnehaha Creek Watershed District
minnehahacreek.org

7

Take a Walk Back to 1850 and Experience the Big Woods

Thanks to the efforts of the Friends of the Big Woods and the citizens of Wayzata, a remnant of what this part of Minnesota once looked like will remain protected for future generations. Big Woods' 14 acres provide a glimpse of the hardwood forest you would have seen here in the days of early settlement.

The woods were a formidable barrier to settlers exploring the Lake Minnetonka. It provided a curtain that kept the lake's secret for so many years. This habitat is precious, with less than 1 percent remaining of the original forest that once stretched across 6,500 square miles of Minnesota.

As part of the terms of the conservation easement, a wood-chip walking trail meanders through the forest of basswood and sugar maples to give visitors up close and personal feel for the land as it once was. Take a moment to sit on a bench and contemplate the story of Lake Minnetonka.

The Big Woods Preserve is located east of the Colonial Square shopping center off of Wayzata Boulevard. It is open all year. Visitors should note that the parking lot is shared with The Retreat treatment center. There is designated trail parking at the entrance. Be assured it is a public park.

Big Woods Preserve
1223 Wayzata Boulevard E, Wayzata
http://www.wayzata.org/Facilities/Facility/Details/Big-Woods-Preserve-30

***

The Ginseng Rush of 1857–1861

While California had its gold, Lake Minnetonka had its ginseng. American ginseng grows wild in rich habitat, such as the Big Woods. According to the folklore, ginseng increases physical performance and mental clarity. If you've ever had a can of Ginseng Rush soda, you probably can relate.

The plant is said to be "*adaptogenic*," meaning it helps the body return to a normal state. Traditional Chinese medicine refers to American ginseng as the yin to Asian ginseng's yang.

During this time, ginseng was still abundant in the Big Woods. A whole industry developed around its harvest, drawing more settlers and the unemployed to the area. Workers received 6 cents a pound for ginseng. In today's money, that is about $1.60.

From the Big Woods, harvesters transported their spoils to Wayzata where it continued its journey to St. Paul by ox cart. To give you an idea of the size of the market, one account placed the 1859 harvest at $2 million, making Minnesota a leader in the industry. The harvest amounted to over 200,000 pounds.

The market changed after its short run. As you might expect, the ginseng market peaked and then crashed, following the pattern of what happened in New England where harvesters exhausted their supply.

It's not to be unexpected with a plant that is harvested for its root. And the leaves have little value. Remove the root, lose a plant. The state of Minnesota stepped in to protect the plant with the Ginseng Law of 1865—after the proverbial horse had fled the barn.

8

Walk, Bike, or Roller Blade the Dakota Trail

The 13-mile Dakota Trail runs from Wayzata to St. Bonifacius, where it connects up with an additional 12.5 miles to Mayer. Though much of its path is through populated areas, you'll be treated to stunning views and glimpses of the cottages of old along the way. The 10-foot wide trail has a gentle slope of 0 to 2 percent grade, making it an ideal choice for young bicyclists. It is one of the few paved trails around.

You can begin at its trail head in Wayzata. Other parking areas include 5515 Lynwood Blvd in Mound, Gale Woods Farm in Minnetrista, at 4150 Bell St in St. Bonifacius, or in Mayer at State Highway 25 and First Street Northwest. Pack a lunch or stop at a restaurant along the way. The Dakota Trail is a popular destination, especially on weekends. A shout out of *"On your left!"* is appreciated.

Note: The trail is not maintained for winter use in some areas.

Dakota Rail trail Head
175 Grove Lane, Wayzata
24/7 Trail Hotline: 763-559-6778

***

Why stop there?

You can continue your exploration of the Lake Minnetonka by following the myriad of nearby trails. Included are major trails in the area. However, many smaller offshoots and local trails exist. Be sure to follow all posted rules.

Three Rivers Park District Trails

Lake Minnetonka LRT Regional Trail
Length: 15 miles
Location: Between Hopkins and Carver Park Reserve

Luce Line Regional Trail
Length: 9 miles

MN Department of Natural Resources

Luce Line State Trail
Length: 63 miles
Plymouth to Winsted: Limestone surface, 30 miles
Winsted to Hutchinson: Paved, 33miles
Snowmobiles permitted west of Stubb's Bay Road

State of Minnesota Recreation Rules
https://www.revisor.mn.gov/rules/?id=6100
Horse passes and a snowmobile state sticker are required on the Luce
Line Trail
Only groomed trails require a ski pass

From the MN DNR site:
http://www.dnr.state.mn.us/state_trails/luce_line/index.html

9

Tour the Wayzata Depot

The simple English Tudor style Wayzata Depot represents a significant time in the life of the village of Wayzata. Completed in 1906, it is a symbol of the truce between the village and James J. Hill.

The depot was state-of-the-art for its time, offering indoor plumbing and steam heat. It served the rail until passenger service ceased in 1971. Despite its heavy use, the Wayzata Depot remains a reminder of the heady days of tourism and commuter traffic.

In 1981, the National Register of Historic Places recognized the Wayzata Depot for its significant place in Wayzata history. The site now serves as the location for the Wayzata Historical Society and the Wayzata Area Chamber of Commerce.

The depot takes you back in time to the days of the flourishing railroad industry. As you walk into what was the waiting area, you can view a time line of Wayzata history along with other relics of the past. The office, the hub of activity of the depot, has several more exhibits, including an interactive display for sending a Morse code message.

But you won't want to stop there. The outside gardens offer a delightful place to sit and enjoy the water and the boats. And you won't want to miss Minnesota's first public garden railroad display. If you feel like walking around, stroll the docks for more scenic views. During the summer, Excelsior's streetcar boat, the *Minnehaha,* docks here. Want to be on the water? Be sure and be at the docks before noon to catch the hour-long round-trip excursion.

Did' You Know? Wayzata pulled out all the stops for its 75th anniversary party for the Wayzata Depot. The celebration included a re-enactment of James Hill's presentation of the depot to the village. Guests feasted on a 1,500 lb cake in the likeness of the Wayzata Depot. The cake measured 34″ x 72″ x 36″. The ingredients reportedly included 220 pounds of butter and over 3,500 eggs.

402 East Lake Street, Wazyata

952-473-3631

wayzatahistoricalsociety.org

***

Wayzata Walking Tour/Lake Tour

You can take your trip into the nostalgia of Wayzata's early days one step further by taking the Wayzata Walking Tour. Maps are available at the depot or online at the Wayzata Historical Society website.

The 17-stop tour begins at the Wayzata Depot and takes you on a journey of the past with stops at the old Gleason's General Store, Moore Boatworks, and Burying Hill, Wayzata's first cemetery.

Prefer a lake tour instead? Follow the 7-stop tour that delves more deeply into Wayzata's past with stops at the historic Arlington Hotel site and Spirit Knob at Breezy Point. You can have your history both ways, on land or water!

10

See Lookout Point

Lookout Point is significant for what it is today and what doesn't exist anymore. The site marks the north shore of the entrance into Wayzata Bay from the water. In 1882, the Minnetonka Yacht Club formed. The club used to run races from Breezy Point, south east of this site. Later, the club moved the starting point to Lookout Point. One look and you'll see why its appropriately named with its scenic view of the lower lake.

But Lookout Point has its place in history for another reason. It once was the site of the grand Frank Peavy's Highcroft mansion. Built in 1895, this magnificent estate stood on a 160-acre site and included a working farm for Peavy's Jersey cattle. Like many who settled in the Ferndale area, Peavy made his fortune in grain.

His 30-room Highcroft mansion with its grand hall and outstanding gardens was a showcase on Lake Minnetonka. The mansion is significant in Lake Minnetonka history as a year-round home. Many of the so-called summer cottages around the lake were for seasonal use only. Highcroft remained in the family after being inherited by Peavy's daughter, Lucia and her husband.

But, like other of the grand homes on the lake, Highcroft wouldn't last long. In 1953, the house was razed, and the land divided into lots for a subdivision.

Note: Lookout Point is private

Location: Point separating Lower Lake North on the east and Smith's Bay on the west

***

Snapshot of the 1860s

- 1860: First school in Mound built at site of the Gillespie Center
- 1860: The first wagon road was legally established in Minnetonka Township called Harrington Road. You might recognize it as Ferndale Road today
- 1860: First steamboat, *Governor Ramsey*, arrives in Wayzata
- 1862: Homestead Act passed. You could claim 160 acres with a stipulation to live on it for five years to get patent on land
- 1865: Wayzata gets its current spelling
- 1867: J. J. Hill's St. Paul and Pacific Railroad connected the Twin Cities with Wayzata
- 1868: The lake's second steamer, the *Sue Gardiner*, launched

11

Slow Down and Relax at the Norenberg Gardens

The Norenberg Gardens mark the home of Grain Belt Brewery founder, Frederick Noerenberg, and his family. It is a true masterpiece of horticulture, with a bloom schedule that reflects native, annual, and perennial plants. And it offers a seasonal display of blooming plants, so it will be different every time you see it. Head over to the gazebo for picture-worthy views of the lake.

The site puts on several events throughout the year, including its Sundays in the Garden and Tuesday evening Garden Tours. Be sure to come back in August to buy some of the site's stunning daylilies for your own garden during its annual Daylily Sale. Please call or check with out the Norenberg Gardens website for time and dates on its event calendar.

Lora Noerenberg Hoppe, one of Norenberg's five children, donated the property to the Three Rivers Park District in 1972. The donation had specific guidelines for the land, including razing of the family home. Please note that food and beverages are not permitted on site. And Fido won't be able to join you on your garden tour.

Norenberg Gardens
2865 Northshore Drive, Wayzata
763-559-6700
threeriversparks.org

***

The Loss of the Estates

Things come and go, but perhaps there are none as astonishing as the loss of the great estates that once existed around Lake Minnetonka. The razing of the Norenberg Estate was hardly an isolated incident.

Did You Know? The Norenberg Estate barn has been nominated for inclusion in the National Register of Historic Places as an example of one of the "gentleman farms" of the era.

Francis Little House, Deephaven (1914-1972)
Designed by Frank Lloyd Wright. Dismantled.

Highcroft Estate, Wayzata (1895-1953)
160-acre estate with a 30-room mansion and 40 by 60 foot great hall and a dairy. Razed in 1953.

Norenberg Estate, Orono (1890-1972)
73-acre estate. Razed in 1972.

Olaf Searle Home, Big Island (1891-1932)
125-acre estate with a 21-room mansion. Razed.

Harold W. Sweatt House, Wayzata (1875-2007)
77-acre estate. Demolished in 2007, and the property subdivided

12

Enjoy a Night of Music at the Wayzata Summer Concert Series

Enjoy the perfect mid-week break with a summer evening concert. The City of Wayzata offers a month-long series of concerts held in Wayzata's Depot Park on Wednesday evenings in July. You can make it a Lake-Minnetonka-kind-of-day with an excursion on Excelsior's streetcar boat, the *Minnehaha,* to the concert. See # 51 in Excelsior for more information.

And the fun doesn't stop here. Get deals and good food during Wayzata Wednesdays, June 1st through August 31. Each month will feature a special event. Visit the chamber website for more details.

Depot Park
402 East Lake Street, Wayzata
952-473-9595
wayzatachamber.com

***

Minnetonka in Song and Verse

Songs
By the Waters of Minnetonka by Thurlow Lieurance*
From the Land of Sky-Blue Waters by Charles Wakefield Cadman

Poems
Minnetonka by Hanford Lennox Gordon
The Song of Hiawatha by Henry Wadsworth Longfellow
Indian Legends and Other Poems by Hanford L. Gordon

*Thurlow Lieurance published the song, *By the Waters of Minnetonka*, in 1913. However, in may 1926, he announced plans to visit the lake area for the first time while traveling in Minneapolis.

Did You Know? The Smithsonian has 21 photographs and 23 paintings featuring scenes of Lake Minnetonka and the surrounding landscape in its collection.

13

Immerse Yourself in Fine Art at the Wayzata Art Experience

The Wayzata Art Experience is just that, an experience. It is a juried art show that encompasses the whole art world. In addition to fine art of all kinds, you'll find some beautiful things to eat and drink too, with gourmet food trucks and vendors crafting their art too.

And the feasts for the eyes don't stop there. You'll find garden art on display too with works by landscape designers and artists. Boaters will love the antique and classic boat show held in conjunction with the event. Live entertainment will complete your experience. Held the last Saturday and Sunday in June.

Wayzata Chamber of Commerce
402 East Lake Street, Wayzata
952-473-9595
wayzataartexperience.com

***

The History of the Wayzata Movie Theater

Like Excelsior, Wayzata had its own iconic movie theater. Opened in 1932, the Wayzata Movie Theater was a popular attraction to say nothing of its one-of-a-kind Art Deco marquee. When it first opened, a movie ticket and popcorn could set you back 35 cents. It's easy to appreciate being able to bring snacks into the theater in its early years.

And if you needed to cool off, its water mist air-conditioning system did the trick. But unlike the Tonka Theater/Excelsior Dock Cinema, the Wayzata Movie Theater didn't last, closing in 1985. While the marquee in town is a replica, it lets the memories live on.

14

Visit the Heritage Park

Heritage Park in Wayzata, known by the ol' timers as Batson's Corner, is a small, but quaint park with perennial gardens and an Armed Forces Memorial. The park is a fitting tribute to the land and its people, including the Batson family who farmed this land until 2000. Visit the park on Veteran's Day and Memorial Day to attend ceremonies those who served in the military, past and present.

Corner of Wayzata Boulevard and Central Avenue, Wayzata

***

Why, What?

In the course of writing this book, I came across oodles of variations on the spelling of Wayzata. To begin, the name is said to mean north shore or a reference to the northern god who blows cold wind out of his mouth. As far as pronunciation, one interpretation comes from the Dakota language as Way-Zay-Tay.

It's worth noting that during this time that white settlers were in the process of translating the language of the Dakota and other American Indians. Stephen Return Riggs and Dr. Thomas Williamson first completed a Dakota grammar and language dictionary in 1852. However, it was a phonetic work, which accounts for the variations you'd encounter back then.

Among the spellings I found were:

- Wy-ze-a-ta
- Wa-zi-ya-ta
- Whyazetta
- Wyzata
- Wyzetta
- Wyzatty
- Wayzetty

In the end, you can thank J.L. Woolnough, a conductor for the Great Northern Railroad, for the current pronunciation of Wayzata. Woolnough wanted to put an end to the confusion, giving the town's its iconic name.

Did You Know? To the American Indians, the North, denoted by the color red, means the hardships endured, followed by the cleansing one receives through this experience. It teaches lessons of patience and endurance.

15

See the Trapper's Cabin at Shaver Park

Shaver Park is located on Grove Lane off of Lake Street. The gently rolling landscape includes picnic areas with grills, a sand volleyball court, and plenty of benches to take in the lake view. The highlight is the old Trapper's Cabin, a restored tamarack-log structure donated to the city in 2012.

Originally in the Big Woods on Bushaway Road, the cabin is likely the lone survivor of this construction. Visitors are sure to be surprised to learn that cabins like this one were the typical home for early settlers to Lake Minnetonka.

To stake their 160-acre claim, the settlers had to show occupancy by clearing the land. They had to build a 8 foot by 10 foot cabin with a door and a window, like what you see here. Also, the land must be surveyed. Then, of course, the government must be paid its share of $1.25 per acre.

James Shaver, a master carpenter from Pennsylvania, came to Lake Minnetonka in 1850. Shaver lived in a claim shanty before building what would become the first boarding house on Lake Minnetonka for the mill crew. He sent for his wife, Sarah Chowen Shaver, to cook for the men.

But, wait! There's more! Walk the trail to the walking bridge where you'll find summer rentals for water sports. Continue to Wayzata Beach (#3), with its beach house with public restrooms, and more chairs to watch the boats go by.

On-street parking available on Lake Street and at the Dakota Trail trailhead (#8). Kiosks include maps of the trail and other recreation areas in the surrounding areas to get your bearings.

Shaver Park
220 Grove Lane E, Wayzata

***

Railroad History

Let's begin by putting the railroad in perspective. Before 1867, settlers had a tough journey to get to Lake Minnetonka. Travel by walking meant going through a maze of marshes, ponds, wetlands, and of course, the Big Woods.

If you think the roads are bad now, travel back then wasn't easy. The first stagecoaches wouldn't run from Wayzata until 1855. And the US Bureau of Public Roads wouldn't establish Rte. 12 to Wayzata until 1925.

The first train rolled into town on the St. Paul and Pacific Railway tracks in 1867, having been finished the day before. As you can imagine, the event drew crowds to watch the *St. Cloud No. 7* pulling in with its single passenger car. At the time, it was literally the end of line.

Horses turned the locomotive around on a turntable to make the return journey. And so began a legacy which would change the Lake Minnetonka area forever. After Wayzata, Excelsior got rail service in 1881, followed by Spring Park in 1890. Mound was last to get in on the game in 1900.

The railroads seized the opportunities to increase ridership. In 1883, the Motor Line launched its Owl Train, which left Excelsior at 10 p.m. And then in 1875, James Hill's St. Paul and Pacific Railroad added scheduled a special train that left the city at 4:30 a.m. and returned at 6:30 p.m. Its purpose was to accommodate city sportsmen who wanted extra time to bag another one or toss a line in a few more times.

Did You Know? Bad roads were a way of life—even back in the 19th century. An early account from the *Lake Minnetonka Tourist* lamented about the rail journey, "*The last five miles at the Wayzata end are enough to shake the life out of a man.*"

16

Take the Lake Minnetonka Trolley

Ride the Lake Minnetonka Trolley. The free service runs Tuesdays and Thursdays from 10 a.m. to 4 p.m. with 16 stops along the way, all within city limits. It runs on the hour from June 14 to September 1. Visit lakefront sites such as the Wayzata Village shops and Wayzata Beach.

While not a tour in the traditional sense, you can easily get around in Wayzata and have a day of fun and exploration. The trolley will make stops during the Wednesday Evening Concert Series.

Reneeslimousines.com

***

Just Your Average Lake

- Average depth: 25.1 feet
- Average depth at sea level from 5/30/1906 through 11/29/2012: 928.45 ft (normal: 929.4 ft)
- Average ice-out date: April 15

- Average weight of largemouth bass, based on 2014 MN DNR gill net survey: 1.03 pounds

- Average weight of muskellunge, based on 2014 MN DNR gill net survey: 15.59 pounds

- Average Annual evaporation from the lake: 30 inches

- Average ice thickness: between 20 and 24 inches

17

Chilly Open!

Think golf is just a fair weather sport? Think again! Get your golf fix on at the Chilly Open's open frozen golf event. Bring your clubs or hockey stock! Get challenged on any of three 9-ice hole courses. Your admission to the event includes live music, prizes, giveaways, and all-you-can-eat chili. Chili, chilly, get it?

But it's not just about golf. Watch snow kite races. Or pack your skates and skate up a storm on the Wayzata Bay luminary rink. You can even take in a movie while you enjoy your chili. Not into golf? How about some frozen yoga on the ice? Don't knock it until you've tried it.

Note: While the event doesn't include alcohol, you can still bring something to take a wee bit of the chill off—as long as you enjoy while on the ice **only**.

Greater Wayzata Chamber of Commerce
wayzatachillyopen.com

***

Places to Eat by Town

Wayzata
Sakana Sushi and Asian Bistro, sakanamn.com
Gianni's*, giannis-steakhouse.com
Cov*, covwayzata.com
The Muni (Wayzata Bar and Grill), wayzatabarandgrill.com
6Smith*, 6smith.com
McCormick's Pub and Restaurant*, mccormickswayzata.com
D'Amico & Sons, 952-476-8866

Orono
Narrow's Saloon, thenarrowssaloon.com

Spring Park
Minnetonka Drive-In, minnetonkadrivein.com
Tonka Grill and Barbecue, tonkagrillandbbq.com
Lord Fletcher's, lordfletchers.com

Mound
Surfside Bar and Grill, 952-283-1136
Scotty B's, scottyb.com
Dakota Station, 952-479-1519
Carbones, carbonespizzeria.com

Shorewood
Hazellewood, hazellewoodgrill.com
Joey Nova's, joeynovas.com

Tonka Bay
The Caribbean, 952-474-3550

Excelsior

Yumi's, yumissushibar.com
Coalition, coalitionrestaurant.com
Haskell's, haskellsport.com
Jake O'Connor, jakeoconnors.com
Lago Tacos, lagotacos.com
The Suburban, thesuburbanmn.com
Olives, olivesfresh.com
Maynards, maynardsonline.com
Bayside Grille, 952-474-1113
318 Cafe, three-eighteen.com
Miyabi, miyabimn.com
Victor's*, victorsonwaterstreet.com

Greenwood

Cast & Cru*, castandcru.com

Denotes more formal dining

PART II

Orono

Visitors to Orono might be puzzled by its curious names. Early settler, George A. Brackett of Maine, named the point on which he lived after his own hometown, Orono. Residents later embraced the name for the town.

Orono began as a part of Excelsior Township, which included acreage on the northern and southern shores of Lake Minnetonka. Likely, you can see the handwriting on the wall. In March 1868, the split of the north and south was complete, with the former becoming part of Medina.

Like other villages, residents struggled with the changing landscape and economics of the lake. They remained concerned about what their role would be in its future. In 1889, Orono came into existence, establishing its own identity in midst of the increasing tourism industry. Signs of the city mention Navarre. Navarre is a name from the town's history that has stuck over the years. It refers to a stop on the Great Northern railroad between Minnetonka Beach and Spring Park.

18

See Bracketts Point

Named after George A. Brackett of Maine, Brackett's Point is located in Lower Lake North, south of Tanager Lake. Brackett purchased the land once called Starvation Point in 1880. The earlier name was a reference to a story about a trapper that allegedly died from starvation on the point.

The Brackett's boys proved the story may have had some truth to it. They found a cabin and a human skull on the property. Brackett named the point, Orono Point, which comes from a town by the same name in Maine on the Penobscot River and the home of the University of Maine. Later, it became simply, Brackett's Point.

Before moving to Lake Minnetonka, George Brackett was an important figure in Minneapolis as part of the first city council and later mayor. He was also a compassionate man. While living in Minneapolis, he provided funding for a hostel for the city's poor. His legacy of community involvement continued on the lake. Like Hazen Burton from Deephaven, he helped form the Minnetonka Yacht Club, becoming its first commodore.

But life on Lake Minnetonka doesn't always mean peace and tranquility. At no time was this more clear than on July 12, 1885, with the sinking of the *Minnie Cook*. She capsized when caught in a gale. Despite what may have been warmer water temperatures, many people at this time simply did not know how to swim. Even today, a lack of swimming ability is a factor in about 34 percent of drownings, according to the US Coast Guard.

Word got out quickly about the accident, with over 100 boats assisting with the grisly recovery. The tragedy took the lives of 10 people. The victims included Alonzo Rand, the former Minneapolis mayor and one of the founders of the Minneapolis Gas Light Company, and four members of his family.

George Brackett showed his compassion once again, assisting with the somber task of recovering the dead. The funeral procession of eight hearses and about 400 black carriages drew over 70,000 mourners. Though hard to believe after this tragedy, the *Minnie Cook* sailed again and almost went down a second time.

Note: Bracketts Point is on private property. Best by water

Did You Know? The streetcar boat, *Hopkins*, operated as an excursion boat after 1926 when the boats stopped running. The new owner changed its name to *Minnetonka*. It remained on the lake until 1944. The boat was sunk near Brackett's Point.

Location: Between Smiths Bay and Lower Lake North

***

Snapshot of the 1870s

- 1873: The Narrows between the lower and upper portions of the lake was widened so that steamboats could pass

- 1873: The four-year grasshopper plague begins

- 1876: Mound City is built

- 1876: Chapman House in Mound opens

- 1877: First explosion on steamer on the lake occurred when the boiler of the *Katie May* exploded, taking three lives. It would later become the *Saucy Kate* excursion boat the following year

- 1877: First village election in Excelsior, which would make the village dry

- 1879: St. Louis Hotel in Deephaven opens

- 1879: Lake Park Hotel in Tonka Bay opens

19

Have a Picnic on Big Island!

Have a picnic in the tradition of how tourists enjoyed the island back in the day. Public docks on the south side of the island offer easy access. It's definitely the quieter side, with the north side being the famous boating tie-up section.

Be sure and bring mosquito repellent and a pair of binoculars. Keep an eye out for the eagles nest here. Leashed pets are welcome. *Note:* alcohol and glass containers are prohibited.

In its heyday, there were two modern kitchen shelters that groups could reserve and four public picnic kitchens. They had all the conveniences needed for a picnic on the island: drinking water, storage, and stoves. Ice and fuel were free. You might wander the grounds, perhaps talking in a concert at the Music Casino. And of course, there was the Big Island Amusement Park.

Note for First-Time Boaters: The waters around Big Island are unusual because of the many navigation buoys around it. Big, after all, doesn't just refer to the island; it also describes the crowds. Make sure you know what each buoy means to safely navigate.

Note: Please stay in designated park areas. Parts of the island are private.

Did You Know? Orono had its own hermit named Samuel Wetherald who befriended the local children.

Location: Big Island

***

The History of Big Island

Big Island wasn't always known by that name. In fact, it's had several different ones through the years. The American Indians called it *Wetutanka*, meaning the *"springtime move to sugaring camp."* They traveled here to tap the trees for maple syrup. The first settler on the island was Judge Bradley Meeker who lived there in 1852. The island became known as Meeker Island.

Later, William Bradford Morse built the first house on the island in 1855 after acquiring the island with his brother, John V. Morse, the previous year. Perhaps an early sign of the recreational spot it would become, he subdivided the land and ran an island campground. But things didn't always go well for Morse. In 1880, he was convicted of selling liquor without a license.

And that wasn't his only brush with the law. The Morse brothers also happened to be uncles of the infamous Lizzie Borden. Yes, *that* Lizzie Borden. Lizzie's father had married Sarah Anthony Morse. Three years after she died in 1863, her father, Andrew, married his second wife, Abby Durfee Gray, Lizzie's stepmother.

Sometime during the morning of August 4, 1892, the ax murders of her father and stepmother occurred in Fall River, Massachusetts. The night before the murder, John Morse had been visiting the Lizzie, an action considered odd for a man who had little contact with the family. His appearance attracted the attention of the police investigating the case, who considered him a *"person of interest"* for a time. John Morse later testified at the trial.

But Morse wasn't the only resident of the island. In 1891, Norwegian, Olaf Searle, bought 125 acres on the north shore of the 275-acre island. Searle had made his fortune helping others migrate to America. Big Island equals big plans. He built a 21-room, 3-story mansion meant for year-round use. It became the first home with steam heat and gas lights. His estate also included a goldfish pond and a Japanese garden.

Having made his fortune in real estate, Searle made living large a life's work. He owned a steam yacht, the *Ralph* and a sailing yacht, the *Dagmar*. Ralph and Dagmar were the names of Searle's son and wife, respectively. Even the boathouse and gazebo were large. After all, what's a gazebo without an orchestra? And that channel between the parts of the island?

Searle had the channel dug out, creating his own island, Mahpiyata Island, accessible by bridge from Big Island. The name means *"celestial peace maiden,"* said to be from a Dakota legend. The rumor was Searle fancied having a moat around his land. But all things come to an end as the saying goes. Searle later lost his fortune and the grand island paradise he created. The mansion burned down not long after it was abandoned.

The next chapter in the history of Big Island includes an aviary, a 200-foot tower, and a casino. Sounds like a walks-into-a-bar joke, doesn't it? Swing on over to #53 for the rest of the story.

20

Rock On at the Narrows Saloon

Established in 1999, the Narrows Saloon is an institution in Orono. It is a destination spot for blues music lovers, featuring live music every day but Mondays.

If you like tequila, you'll love their extensive choice of fine pours. A little too much partying over the weekend? Be sure to try out their Hangover Bennie, just one of the choices on their weekend breakfast menu.

Did You Know? The intersection of Cty Rd 15 and Cty Rd 19 was once known as Jackson's Corner. At the time, Cty. Rd. 15 was called Cty. Rd. 7.

3380 Shoreline Dr, Wayzata

952-471-3352

thenarrowssaloon.com

***

The Making of a Channel

The Narrows Channel wasn't always the Narrows Channel. It wasn't even in the same place. You'll have to look for # 46 south of the Narrows in Tonka Bay to see the original one. In 1883, Captain Johnson's dredging company dredged the Narrows Channel we know today so that steamboats could get through. And not just the smaller ones, but the mother of all steamboats, the 300-foot, 2,500-passenger *Belle of Minnetonka*.

And it wasn't alway called the Narrows, but rather Hull's Narrows, named after Stephen Hull, a Universalist preacher. Hull built his cabin on Crystal Creek near what was the old channel in 1853. He had enlarged the creek to allow for passage between the upper and lower lakes.

Hull was the first white settler in Excelsior Township. At one time, only one way existed to get to the upper lake. The lack of more navigable thoroughfare stood in the way of the growth of the booming Lake Minnetonka tourist industry. Before 1865, the stage coach provided the only way to travel from Minneapolis to Wayzata. The rest of the Lake Minnetonka area was wilderness and makeshift trails cut through the Big Woods and wetlands.

Mound City wanted to get a piece of the pie since it was virtually cut off from the rest of Lake Minnetonka. It wasn't unusual at that time for boats to get stuck in the mud and muck of the channel which varied in depth between three and five feet. It gave a whole new meaning to the phrase, log jam.

And if that wasn't enough, fluctuating water levels with dry summers and the dam at Minnetonka Mills added to the frustration. Before dredging, the 40-acre area was filled with wild rice. It served as a channel for smaller boats and certainly not steamboats or steamers as they were called. Finally, the Minnesota state legislature allocated funds for improvement. The channel was moved to the present location at the Narrows Channel. Boat traffic became more tolerable. But then came the issues with automobile and foot traffic.

For a time, the county set up a cable ferry to get traffic across the water between Minnetonka Lake Park (Tonka Bay) and Navarre. The ferryboat was a wooden flat boat about 25 feet long. And the Narrows managed well for a time, even handling the traffic from the largest of the steamers, the *Belle of Minnetonka* and the *City of St. Louis.*

But as tourist traffic grew, so did the bottlenecks. Some accounts suggest traffic jams approaching 100 vehicles of all sorts. At one point, a drawbridge was proposed to ease the traffic woes. Help finally came in 1911 with funds to build a modern bridge. However, the county board soon found itself between the proverbial rock and a hard place over the bridge.

The yacht club thought the bridge was too low at 24 feet. The cottage owners, on the other hand, sued, complaining it was too high, and that it obstructed their view of the lake and decreased their property values.

After more bickering, scandals, and calls for the removal of the county board, the matter was settled, and the bridge that was just right was built. It would later be replaced and dedicated in 1964. But, it certainly wasn't the end of conflicts on the lake.

PART III

Minnetonka Beach

The city of Minnetonka Beach, affectionately know as "*The Beach*," lies between Crystal Bay to the north and west and Lafayette Bay on the south. The first settlers came to the area in 1855, but its wasn't platted until 1883. The village's most famous building was the Hotel Lafayette, built in 1882 by railway baron, James J. Hill.

When the hotel tragically burned down in 1897, the land was parceled out into 193 individual lakefront lots. The shoreline of each one formed a common property to all community residents. When the lots first sold at auction, they fetched between $300 and $800 each. In today's money, the cost would be about $8,615 to $22,975, a steal worth seeking.

The whole village was seasonal. As late as 1898, the town remained uninhabited between November and the middle of April. But, this seasonal lifestyle would soon change. An account from 1906 expressed surprise at the notion of residents living in Minnetonka Beach all year and commuting to Minneapolis to work.

By 1997, Minnetonka Beach had evolved into a year-round community, with only the Thompson Summer House standing as a remnant of its past.

21

Recall the Glamor of the Hotel Lafayette

Though no remnants of the original hotel exist, you can still see the site where the Hotel Lafayette once stood. This is one of the best-by-water views or via the Dakota Trail which passes right through the club. If you walk or bike the Dakota Trail, you'll follow the path that the trains once took, stopping in front of the hotel. It's a unique way to capture the experience of walking in the footsteps of history.

As you boat through Narrows Channel from Old Channel Bay into Lafayette Bay, look to your left toward the shore. If it were 1882, you'd see the Hotel Lafayette.

Not to be outdone, James Hill had planned his own grand hotel that would rival any on the lake, then or since. In 1882, he opened his five-story Hotel Lafayette, at a cost of $815,000. The hotel was grand in every sense of the word.

Built on 700 acres, it had 300 rooms with modern amenities such as electric lights. Its stunning views of Crystal and Lafayette Bays matched the splendor of its three grand staircases. (The Lafayette Bay had been called Holmes Bay at the time.)

Hill realized his vision to create the largest hotel. At 745 feet, it was nearly twice the size of its rival, the Lake Park Hotel. For its grand opening, Hill oversaw every last detail down to the music that the orchestra played. And you thought your boss was a micro-manager.

Hill employed 150 people to carry out the operations of his behemoth. The highlight of the opening was the launch of this steamboat, the 2,500-passenger *Belle of Minnetonka*. The lake would never be the same.

And so it continued its reign of splendor and luxury. The hotel hosted dignitaries and famous people of the time, including General Ulysses S. Grant who visited the hotel twice, President Chester Arthur, and environmentalist, John Muir. The hotel offered luxury but in a style all Hill's own.

His establishment was also known for serving alcohol by the glass, an illegal practice at the time. Yet, despite repeated arrests of his bartender, he continued to see to the comfort and pleasure of his guests, despite what the law said. Talk about taking one for the team.

And of course, the drinking at the hotel didn't go unnoticed by the citizenry either. But perhaps even Hill didn't know the dark path that lay ahead.

A letter on September 17, 1892 by Captain E.A. Holcombe, manager of the Hotel Lafayette, showed the extent of the financial quagmire of the hotel. With nearly $40,000 in the red, its fate was becoming clear. To put that in perspective, $40,000 equals about $1,064,241 in today's money.

Hill knew its demise was inevitable, having considered its sale three weeks prior. The hotel continued to sputter along through the years. Tourism continued to dwindle, with 1893 experiencing a 50 percent drop in business. Some hotels even began closing early for the season.

Following the close of the 1897 season, the rumors began flying of its demise. The stories became a reality when the Hotel Lafayette mysteriously burned down in 1897. No one was injured or killed, thankfully.

Within one hour, the hotel called "*the finest hotel west of New York City*" would be gone forever. Ironically, each room in the hotel had a fire-extinguishing glass grenade to be used in case of a fire.

The thought may have occurred to you that the fire at the Hotel Lafayette smacks of a certain convenience. It occurred during the off season. No one was on site. The water had been turned off. And the fire raced through the structure that had been losing money for years. An article in the *Minneapolis Tribune* wrote that it "*. . . dared not speculate on the cause of the fire.*"

Hill's railroad ventures played a role in the demise of his grand hotels. In the late 1880s into the 1890s, tourists from the South traveled by train, but the Lake Minnetonka area was no longer the destination. Onward meant westward as passengers opted for other tourist destinations such as Yellowstone National Park.

But the story of the Hotel Lafayette had one final chapter. In 1899, James Hill sold a 38-acre parcel of land for what would become the first country club in the area, the Minnetonka Pleasure Club, or as we know it today, the Lafayette Club. Hill became its first honorary member, lending the historic name of his hotel to the club.

The Grand Hotel of Mackinac Island offers a modern-day example of its splendor. Built in 1887, the hotel stands as a remnant of the tradition of opulent hotels. Its 390-rooms provide accommodations for 130,000 guests each year.

Boasting the world's longest porch, the hotel entered the rank of National Historic Landmarks in 1989. Had the Hotel Lafayette survived, we can only speculate if it would have achieved similar fame.

Note: While the Dakota Trail is public, the Lafayette Club is not. Please respect the privacy of the club.

2800 Northview Rd, Minnetonka Beach
Lafayette Bay and Crystal Bay

***

The History of Minnetonka Beach

For a town which only has a total area of 0.5 square miles, several townships claimed it through its history. The town was part of Excelsior Township from 1858 through 1884, part of Medina until 1889. Orono Township also had a portion of Minnetonka Beach. In 1879, the village had its first road surveyed. Then, in 1886, its first wagon bridge was built.

Though the road had been surveyed earlier, it wouldn't be constructed until 1887, leaving village residents with difficult travel options before its construction. To get to Minnetonka Beach, you had to drive around Crystal Bay. You could do this by taking Russell's Pass (Cty Rd. 51) between North and West Arms, assuming you didn't take the train. It's a wee bit easier today.

Did You Know? Minnetonka Beach incorporated in 1894 for the purpose of "*social enjoyment, mental and physical culture.*"

22

Admire the Architecture of St. Martin's-by-the Lake

Just passing by St. Martin's-by-the-Lake Episcopal Church, you know it's something special. Owned by Major George A. Camp, Cass Gilbert designed the chapel in 1881 in *"the seaside style of New England."* Gilbert would later make a name for himself, designing the Minnesota State Capitol and New York City's Woolworth buildings.

Tragically, George and Lucy had lost three children in infancy. Camp had the chapel built as a memorial to them. It was later used for the wedding of his lone surviving daughter, Lucy May, to Henry Wedelstaedt on September 4, 1888.

As the story goes, Major George Camp heard Bishop Gilbert (not the same person) call for land to build a church during a presentation. Camp heeded the call, going step further. He donated his chapel to the Episcopal church and moved it to its present location. He had one condition for his gift: there would be at least 10 Sunday services held each year.

George Camp was an important figure in the lumber industry, beginning as a mill employee. From the time he completed his wartime service, he made a name for himself bringing his knowledge and experience to the industry. In 1875, he was elected to the state legislature where he continued as an advocate for the lumber industry.

In some ways, he wasn't unlike James J. Hill as a leader in his trade. He and Thomas Barlow Walker ran the first and largest steam-powered sawmill. His shrewd business sense allowed him to become of one of the wealthiest men in the area. His legacy continues with his generous donation of the Camp Chapel to the Episcopal Church.

2801 Westwood Road, Minnetonka Beach (Corner of Cty. Rd. 15 and Westwood Road)

***

The Thomson Summer House: A Symbol of a Bygone Era

Even if you don't know its history, the Thomson Summer House stands out. Traveling from Orono to Wayzata along Cty. Rd. 15, you'll see the white and green Thomson Summer House on your left. Ohio lawyer, Charles Telford, and his wife, Kate Harris Thompson, built the house in 1887.

The 2.5-story house with its Queen Anne style windows and asphalt-shingled roof epitomizes a summer house with its open, airy feel. Can't you just picture yourself sitting on its wide screened-in porch, watching the boats on the lake?

When the land was originally purchased, strict restrictions accompanied the sale, including prohibition of alcohol sales and a condition that no "*immoral, unlawful, or disreputable*" resort occupy the site, a thinly disguised reference to James Hill's Hotel Lafayette which had acquired something of a reputation.

The house stands pretty much as it always has, with minor revisions and deletions. Although the carriage house and outdoor privy are long gone, many period elements still exist, including its built-in cupboards and original beadboard ceilings.

Perhaps best of all, it exists as it has meant to for all these years as one of the last remaining representatives of that bygone era. The National Register of Historic Places recognized its unique character in December 1997. The Minnesota Preservation Alliance praised its reconstruction in 2005 which the family completed to stabilize the building.

Note: The Thomson Summer House is a private residence. Look, but don't touch.

3012 Shoreline Drive, Minnnetonka Beach

PART IV

Spring Park

The next stop on your tour of Lake Minnetonka is Spring Park. This 148-acre town was surveyed and platted in 1880. The towns on the west end of the lake are located around the upper lake.

Until the railroad came to Spring Park in 1890, most of these villages remained small. The dense woods and spacious wetlands made them virtually inaccessible. The railroad changed everything.

Spring Park's claim to fame is also linked with James Hill. Built by Hill, the Hotel Del Otero was one of the five grand hotels on Lake Minnetonka. Of all of them, the hotel lasted the longest. Today, Spring Park embraces its recreational opportunities. Whether you like to bike or paddle board, you'll find plenty of ways to enjoy the outdoors.

.

23

Enjoy a Meal at a Lake Minnetonka Tradition, Lord Fletcher's

Like Al and Alma's (#28), Lord Fletcher's Old Lake Lodge is another Lake Minnetonka tradition you shouldn't miss. Opened in 1968, the restaurant offers both casual and fine dining. For a formal meal, visit its main dining room for that rustic lake lodge experience. If casual is more your thing, the Oar Room or the outdoor Wharf will fit the bill, especially on Lobster Wednesdays during the summer.

Lord Fletcher's is more than just dining. And it's one of the few restaurants that has boat docks on the lake. Enjoy live music on the Wharf or in the Oar House. Feeling more athletic? How about joining a volleyball team for the summer or trying your hand at broom ball during the winter? Lord Fletcher's has you covered.

3746 Sunset Drive, Spring Park
952-471-8513
lordfletchers.com

***

Bridging the Gap

Getting across a 14,034-acre lake by land isn't quick by any means. Fortunately, bridges connect the dots and make the trek a wee bit faster. Each of the 18 bridges includes the waters it connects as well as the clearance with normal lake water levels.

If you notice, several bridges such as Boy Scout Bridge have low clearances. If you have a smaller boat, you'll get to explore more of the lake. Sometimes bigger isn't always better.

Arcola: Crystal Bay and Smiths Bay, 14.75′

Black Lake: Black Lake and Spring Park Bay, 9.75′

Boy Scout: Maxwell Bay and West Arm, 7′

Carsons Bay: Carsons Bay, 5.7′

Coffee: Coffee Cove and Crystal Bay, 13.5′

Emerald Lake: Emerald Lake and Cooks Bay, 12.3′

Forest Lake: West Arm and Forest Lake, 11.7′

Grays Bay: Grays Bay and Wayzata Bay, 14.3′

Halsted Bay: Priests Bay and Halsted Bay, 15′

Hendrickson: Crystal Bay and North Arm, 15′

Libbs Lake: Libbs Lake and Grays Bay, 8.8′

Lost Lake: Lost Lake and Cooks Bay, 11.1′

Narrows: Old Channel Bay and Lafayette Bay 18.25′

Noerenberg: Maxwell Bay and Crystal Bay, 12.7′

Seton Lake: Seton Lake and Harrison Bay, 12.7′

St. Albans Bay: Excelsior Bay and St. Albans Bay, 12.5′

Tanager Lake: Tanager Lake and Lower Lake North, 10.2′

Zimmermans Pass: West Upper Lake and Phelps Bay, 11.5′

24

Cruise In!

Have a burger and a root beer at the Minnetonka Drive-In. It is a truly family business. Started by parents, Gordon and Jeanette Bennyhoff, in 1961, the torch has passed to son, Dave, who continues the family tradition of good food. Enjoy daily specials and drive-in favorites like chili dogs. Known for its blast-of-the-past carhop service, the drive-in has become known for its Thursday night Cruise-Ins.

Classic car owners from all around come out to the Minnetonka Drive-In to show off their suped-up rides. The cars start rolling in during the late afternoon hours. You can reach the drive-in either by car or via the Dakota Trail that runs right past the place. It's a must for all car lovers of all ages. Who knows? You may even see a Selby Cobra; I did.

Note: Park across the street from the drive-in to leave more room for the classic cars. Use the crosswalk. The area gets busy during the cruise-in. *Please* exercise caution when crossing the road.

Minnetonka Drive-In
4658 Shoreline Drive, Spring Park
952-471-9383
minnetonkadrivein.com

***

Getting Around Lake Minnetonka for Landlubbers

One of the major barriers to exploring Lake Minnetonka and its settlements in the early days was the lack of good roads. Some might argue the situation persists today. Nevertheless, making one's way through wetlands and woods teeming with mosquitoes and other more formidable foes made travel difficult, to say the least.

Wolves, for example, still roamed this part of Minnesota along with bears and other creatures of the night. Settlers hacked their own roads in the beginning. Harrington Road, or what is now known as Ferndale Road in Wayzata, was the first surveyed road. Others followed, but maybe not as quickly as you might have thought.

It wasn't until 1905 when the state of Minnesota began building roads and bridges with the creation of the State Highway Commission. Before this time, railroads offered the best way to travel. The existing roads in Minnesota were little more than dirt paths like the rest of the country.

Then, in 1916, the federal government began providing funding for states. But even then, things proceeded slowly. Rather than creating new roads, the state focused on fixing the existing ones. It would take the Federal Aid Highway Act of 1944 before a real opportunity to improve secondary roads surfaced.

- 1860: Harrington Road in Wayzata surveyed

- 1879: First road through Minnetonka Beach is surveyed. It wouldn't be built until 1894

- 1888: Manitou Road (Cty Rd 19) was constructed with a ferry boat connecting Tonka Bay and Navarre across the channel

- 1905: Cty Rd. 44 in Mound completed

- 1925: The US Bureau of Public Roads established Rte. 12 from Minneapolis to Wayzata

25

Rent a Bike

The leisurely way to explore Lake Minnetonka is by bicycle. With plenty of trails and low-traffic roads around the area, you can make it a day. There are also several restaurants along the trails to grab a quick snack. Look for the Dakota Station in Mound or the Minnetonka Drive-In in Spring Park. Bayside Bar and Grille or Maynards will fit the bill in Excelsior.

Bike Rentals Around Lake Minnetonka

Black Oar Rentals
4012 Shoreline Dr, Spring Park
952-807-2476
theblackoar.com

South Lake Cycle
344 Water St, Excelsior
952-474-3179
southlakecycle.bike

***

The Towns and Villages of Lake Minnetonka

1853: Excelsior

1854: Wayzata

1859: Minnetrista

1880: Spring Park

1882: Woodland

1889: Orono

1894: Minnetonka Beach

1900: Deephaven

1912: Mound

1956: Greenwood

1956: Shorewood

1901: Tonka Bay

26

Barbecue, Minnetonka style!

When you've had your fun in the sun, head on over to Tonka Grill and Bar-B-Que. Try their delicious, award-winning hometown barbecue. You'll find the restaurant located across the street from the public boat launch. Get your hands on some ribs, chicken, and pork, smoked on-site. With limited dock access, you can head over from the water. Take out available.

4016 Shoreline Drive, Spring Park
952-471-7447
tonkagrillandbbq.com
Closed on Mondays

***

Minnetonka Firsts

- First real hotel on upper lake: Lakeview House, Mound

- First summer hotel on the lake: Harrington Inn, Wayzata

- First road: Harrington Road (now called Ferndale Road), Wayzata

- First family in the area: James and Sarah Chowen Shaver with their son, James in 1852

- First building exclusively for church services: Trinity Episcopal Church in Excelsior

- First house built for summer use: Maplewood Inn in 1869

- First stern wheeler on the lake, the *Hattie May*, completed in 1878

- First Frank Lloyd Wright House in Minnesota: Deephaven, 1915

- First of three hotels in downtown Excelsior, the Appledore located on west side of Water Street near corner of Second Street, 1879

- First railway station on Carsons Bay, Cottagewood, in 1886

- First of the grand hotels to open: Hotel St. Louis in 1879

27

Visist the site of the Hotel Del Otero

Built by James Hill, the Hotel Del Otero opened in 1885 at the site where the Mist Condos exist now. It was a more modest venue than the other grand enterprises of Hill. The Hotel Del Otero fit in with the growing influx of cottagers by renting out cottages of its own like the ones you see east of the condos.

The Sheriff's Water Patrol across the street marks the site of the hotel's casino. No irony there, huh? Its other attractions included a dancing pavilion, bar, restaurant, screened-in piazzas, and picnic grounds. The hotel ran a small boat fleet for guests as well.

The Hotel Del Otero was quite popular, often booking up. A handbook about the lake published in 1901 mentions the hotel's many modern conveniences, including telephones and *"fresh water from the lake."*

It's not too much of a stretch given that Spring Park Bay is one of the A-graded bays on the lake. And it's easy to imagine how guests could be so taken with the hotel and its magnificent views, still awe-inspiring. Perhaps this was among the reasons the Hotel Del Otero outlasted most of the other hotels on the lake.

Like many hotels, a fire took out the Hotel Del Otero during the height of the season. By all accounts, it truly was an unfortunate accident.

Note: The condos, cottages, and of course, the Water Patrol are private. But take a moment to take in the view. You'll understand what made the Hotel Del Otero so popular.

Shoreline Drive, Spring Park Bay

***

Snapshot of the 1880s

- 1880-1881: First railroad tracks through Excelsior built

- 1880: The legendary Arlington House opened in Wayzata

- 1881: The 160-foot sidewheeler, the *City of St. Louis*, is launched

- 1882: Minnetonka Yacht Club opened in 1882, the first inland sailing club in the United States

- 1888: First streetlights in Wayzata

- 1889: The village of Wayzata sued James Hill to remove the railroad from public streets

- 1889: The Minnetonka Yacht Club and the Excelsior Yacht Club merged

.

PART V

Mound

Mound, or Mound City originally, was named for the prominent Indian mounds in the area. An early account refers to the mounds located between Cooks Bay and Langdon Lake in the naming of the village. But before it was called Mound, it was part of the township known as German Home, named for the large numbers of German settlers in the south and west parts of the township.

When the township government organized in 1859, the city fathers voted to change the name of the township to Minnetrista. The name meant water-crooked, in a nod to the number of crooked lakes in the township. Mound City was built in 1876. Early in its settlement, Mound remained isolated, being surrounded by water or wetlands on the east, north, and south sides. The forests and underbrush were dense, making for difficult travel.

The habitat, however, provided the means of the area's rapid growth. The cord wood industry flourished with plenty of maple, oak, and basswood for the taking. Cord wood construction using the harvested wood with masonry and cob, offered a cheap and relatively easy method of construction as well as fuel for the steam locomotives. Barges delivered the harvest from its source to rail stops for transport from the lake. And it helped Mound both from a financial perspective and in its accessibility.

Cooks Bay was the happening place on this side of Lake Minnetonka with its appropriately named Busy Corners intersection nearby. Hotels on the bay attracted tourists and sportsmen to the area. These early hotels included the Chapman House and Lake View House.

During the summer of 1876, tourism was in full swing, with the Chapman House registering 1,000 guests and the Lake View House, 700 guests. Guests traveled to Mound via two steamers, each carrying 75 or more passengers.

With the Bartlett House, Mound City Hotel, Buena Vista, Palmer House, and the Maple Heights Inn and several smaller hotels and boarding houses, Mound fit in well with burgeoning tourism industry. It appealed to guests looking for moderately priced accommodations. Then, there was the Hermitage built by Frank Halstead, considered a retreat of sorts. And of course, there were the mounds, which residents and visitors viewed as a curiosity.

While the railroad came to Spring Park in 1890, tourists still had to walk or take a horse-drawn wagon to get to town. The part of the township known as Mound separated from the township in 1912 at the height of the tourism boon.

This was an interesting time for Mound. The Twin City Rapid Transit Company's express boats made stops on Cooks Bay to bring tourists from Excelsior to the village. Commuting to Minneapolis took on a new flavor back then. You could take an express boat to Excelsior, hop on a train, and get downtown in less than two hours.

During its heyday, upward of 1,500 to 1,600 tourists visited Mound daily. Some visitors built summer cottages around the lake, spending the warmer months here. Many of the villages in the three original townships—Minnetrista, Minnetonka, and Excelsior—followed a similar pattern of growth and expansion. It wasn't long before advertisements of Mound suggested to "… *live in Mound year-round.*"

28

Have a Supper Club Experience at Al and Alma's

Founded in 1956 by the original Al and Alma, Al and Alma's offers a supper club experience—Lake Minnetonka style. Start your meal with the classic basket of rolls and crackers. It has just the kind of dishes you'd expect at a proper supper club: steaks, ribs, and its signature, Camp-Style walleye.

From its early beginnings as the site of Chester Park Grocery Store, the legacy as a local hangout. The original store rented boats and ran a lunch counter from 1920s to 1956. After acquiring the site, Al and Alma Quist remodeled the store and stepped into local history.

In the 1980s, Al and Alma's added summer dinner cruises, bringing back another of the old lake traditions. It later revived the days of motor yachts in the 1990s. Not to be outdone, the owners commissioned what will be the largest motor yacht in Lake Minnetonka History, the 83-Foot *Bella Vista*, a beautiful view of her own right.

Note: While the restaurant is easy to get to on the water, you'll find it quicker using your smartphone's GPS for landlubbers.

5201 Piper Road, Mound
Office: 952-472-3098
al-almas.com

***

The *Belle of Minnetonka*

Formerly known as the *Phil Sheridan* on the Mississippi River, the *Belle of Minnetonka* began her life in 1866 in Cincinnati. James Hill had to have the best. So, he arranged for the mighty steamer to be dismantled and rebuilt on Lake Minnetonka at the site of the present-day Cov Restaurant in Wayzata (#5).

The *Belle of Minnetonka* stood tall among the steamers of her day. Her resume includes many highlights, including a speed record for travel between St. Paul and St. Louis. But it wasn't just the best. It was always the biggest. The *Belle of Minnetonka* had a capacity of an astounding 2,500 passengers, twice that of the second largest steamboat of the day, the *City of St. Louis*. The steamboat had several dining rooms, 40 sleeping berths, and two orchestras.

To say that the *Belle of Minnetonka* and the *City of St. Louis* were rivals would be nothing short of an understatement. They raced each other across the lake. While the *City of St. Louis* had the maneuvering ability, the *Belle of Minnetonka* had the speed.

One account reported that the the *Belle of Minnetonka* ran aground near Breezy Point during one of its races with the its rival. Talk about a wild ride! Imagine today's *Minnehaha* racing one of Al and Alma's charter boats across the lake!

But let's put her size into perspective. Al and Alma's largest boat of their fleet is the 83-foot *Bella Vista*. The *Belle of Minnetonka* was 300 foot long, over four times the size of the *Bella Vista*. But while the Al and Alma's fleet continues to enjoy success, the *Belle of Minnetonka's* story borders tragic.

After the flurry of excitement over her launch, the steamer's days were numbered. Financial troubles of Hill's Lake Minnetonka Navigation Company led to the *Belle of Minnetonka* not running for the entire 1889 season. Several factors had contributed to the fall of tourist traffic, not the least of which were the rise of cottagers and the opening of the West with the railroad.

St. Albans Bay would be the final resting place of the grand *Belle of Minnetonka*. In the fall of 1892, she was dismantled, with her keel destroyed and her boilers, exhaust pipes, and engines salvaged for another boat. Alas, the old girl was no more. But what about her bell, you ask? Check out #61 in Excelsior.

Postscript: On September 20, 2011, A 2012 survey by Maritime Heritage Minnesota recorded an anomaly, roughly 72 foot long in St. Albans Bay. The size and location suggest that it could be the *Belle of Minnetonka*.

29

Stroll the Andrew Sisters Trail

"We were such a part of everybody's life in the Second World War. We represented something overseas and at home, a sort of security."
~Patty Andrews

Thanks to the efforts of Tom Rockvam, the city of Mound is well-acquainted with its famous singers, the Andrew Sisters. Maxene, LaVerne, and Patty grew up here and later summered in Mound after hitting it big in the music business.

From small town girls with a love for music, the trio became America's most popular female vocal group. They surpassed both Elvis Presley and the Beatles with top-ten hits. Some of their signature hits included *Boogie Woogie Bugle Boy, I Can Dream, Can't I?*, and *I'll Be with You in Apple Blossom Time*. And who can forget such timeless classics like the *Beer Barrel Polka* or *Don't Sit Under the Apple Tree?*

It was Tom Rockvam's vision to push to create the trail, commemorating the Andrew Sisters. Working with Patty Andrews, his efforts paid off, recognizing Mound's most famous citizens. Look for the City of Mound plaque at its start.

Down the road from the Intersection of Commerce Blvd and Auditors Road, Mound

***

The Tortured Tale of Lost Lake

The name, Lost Lake, may suggest a story, and you'd be right. Mound/Mound City was a player in the hotel business from the early days. It found its niche with the middle class and sportsmen. But Mound did not have the large docks to receive visitors in town like Excelsior.

In Blanche Nichols Wilson's book, *Minnetonka Story*, she recounts an account by an early settler to Mound, Paul Hessing. He described Mound as *"No roads, not even Indian trails, nothing but trees, vines, underbrush so thick the sun couldn't shine through…There was no evidence that anyone had ever been here."*

The railroad finally reached the village in 1900. Mound got connected to rest of the lake with the addition of phone lines and phone booths in 1902. But there still was a problem.

The city fathers hit upon the idea of the channel across Lost Lake. It could provide a means to connect the train depot with Cooks Bay. It was a welcome day on October 5, 1906 when the channel first opened. Fred Bartlett had the honors of taking his steamer, *Mound*, through it for its inaugural trip.

Like the Narrows, the Lost Lake Channel had its own share of conflict and compromises. It also proved to be more trouble perhaps than anticipated with the high cost of continual dredging. It soon was abandoned.

The channel languished for many years. Then, the city of Mound dredged it again, determined to do it right this time. With the addition of boat access at the city docks, the channel to Lost Lake functions as it did in the day of the hotels. The days of staying the night are over. Yet, visitors can walk the streets and trails around town and stop at one of the city's casual dining restaurants.

Did You Know? Before the glaciers redirected its path, the Mississippi River flowed through Mound.

30

Be a Tourist at Busy Corners

In the days of hotels and tourism, Busy Corners was the hub of Mound, located down the road from the present Commerce Blvd and Shoreline Drive intersection. The hotel era began with the opening of Cook's Lake View House in 1854. Tourism took off slowly until the dredging of Hull's Narrows (#20) opened the way for travel to the upper lake.

By the mid-1880s, roads entered Mound from Spring Park, St. Bonifacius, and Maple Plain, with all roads leading to Busy Corners. Even with the roads as they were, most tourists came by train to Mound in early 1900s.

The corner by Surfside Park saw boat traffic, taking tourists to the hotels located around the shore. Passengers walked or were later met by car or wagon at the depot. To stroll from the intersection at Commerce Blvd and Shoreline Drive to Surfside Park is a step back in time to Mound's days as a popular tourist stop.

Commerce Blvd and Shoreline Drive, Mound

***

Mound Hotel History

Mound's hotels capitalized on what it offered that the grand hotels could not. Like most hotels on this end of the lake, the most were smaller venues with fewer rooms. But that is precisely what made these hotels popular. Health and comfort were important draws, which was clear in many of the period advertisements.

Dewey House on Cooks Bay boasted of its *"clean air and good times."* Sunset View Villa advertised, *"Always Cool."* The 1889 *Health Magazine* praised the Palmer House as a *"healthful resting place"* and a sanitarium for hayfever patients.

A 1893 guide of the lake reported that *"Travelers from every clime gather at Minnetonka to gain health and strength from her rich, bracing air and pure water."* A 1917 map of the Cities of Lakes, Rivers, and Parks published by the Twin Cities lines boosted that the *"death rate in the Twin Cities is lower than that of any other large community in the United States."* That's a cheery thought to keep in mind when planning your Lake Minnetonka visit.

While the Hotel Lafayette had its glamor, Mound hotels offered a respite on the quiet side of the lake. With less traffic at this end, visitors relaxed and enjoyed the lake in all its simplicity. Several hotels stand out as beacons of the time.

The Cook's House ushered the way for Mound's hotel history, opening in 1854. The 50-room Chapman House and ground opened its doors on July 4, 1876, advertising the *"finest fishing grounds in Mound,"* according to a 1930 travel guide.

Not to be outdone, owner, Ed D. Bartlett, claimed that his hotel was "... *one of the best fishing resorts in Minnesota.*" And of course, there was the Hotel Buena Vista, another sportsmen favorite. You can see a photograph of the hotel from its heyday at the Walgreens Store at Shoreline Drive and Commerce Blvd.

J.H. Woolnough, a conductor for the Great Northern Railroad, owned the Maple Heights Inn. Woolnough, you might remember from earlier in this book, has his place in history as the one who decided on the pronunciation of Wayzata. Except for the Maple Heights Inn, the hotel industry died out by the 1920s. And as for the good fishing in Cooks Bay? I'll leave that for you to decide.

Bartlett House (1883-1926)

Chapman House (1876-1912)

Cook's Lake View House (1854-1912)

Dewey House (1899-Apartment house burned down 1985)

Harrow House (1879-?)

Hotel Buena Vista (1903-1926)

Hotel Harrow, Shady Island (1880-?)

Maple Heights Inn/Woolnoughs/Tippiwauken: Island Park (1880s-1964)

Mound City Hotel (1884-1924)

Palmer House in Zumbra Heights (1899?)

Sunset View Hotel (1908-?)

Switzerland Hotel (1910?)

Note: The history of the Mound hotels has many gaps as the list shows. However, the stories live on in the folks that visited these places.

31

Shop the Farmers' Market

Started in 2009, the Mound Farmers' Market offers a good choice of fresh produce, baked goods, and more. Located along the Dakota Trail, you can make it a stop for picking up fresh salad ingredients as you ride the trail. There is plenty of free parking. You can even boat to the market. The public docks on Lost Lake are within walking distance.

The market is a non-profit organization and managed by a volunteer board committee. Have your own produce to sell? Apply to set up your own market space for the full season or just for a month.

5515 Shoreline Drive, Mound
Saturdays 8:30am -12:30pm
moundfarmersmarketandmore.org

***

Why Stop There? More Farmers Markets on the Lake

Of course, Mound isn't the only farmers' market around Lake Minnetonka. In addition to the small family-run sites, the cities around the lake have plenty of fresh produce and more to offer. Conveniently, they run on different days, so you can stock up all week long.

Did You Know? The Minnesota Cottage Foods Law requires that anyone selling cottage foods like pickles or jams must take food safety training and register with the Minnesota Department of Agriculture. The food must be labeled with the name and address of the seller, the date produced, and the ingredients, including potential allergens. And the person selling it must be the one who made it. That includes products sold on the Internet too.

Wayzata
Thursdays, 1 p.m. to 5 p.m.
763-238-2702
http://minnesotagrown.com/member/wayzata-farmers-market/

Excelsior
Tuesdays, 2 p.m. to 6 p.m.
http://mfma.org/pages/ExcelsiorFarmersMarket/

32

Go to the Dogs at Dog Days Westonka

What better way to celebrate the dog days of summer than going to the dogs! Held in August, the Dogs Days Westonka is all about our canine friends. Browse through the pet expo of pet products and services. Watch the pet parade and the blessing of the animals. Yes, ladies, you can bring your husbands.

And what doggie event wouldn't be complete without a cutest puppy contest? The event is free, but a pet food donation is requested. You don't even need to bring a dog. Come by to see the pets and get your puppy fix.

5515 Shoreline Drive, Mound
westonkacc.com/dog-days-westonka

***

A Brief History of Tonka Toys

Other than the Indian mounds, another thing synonymous with the city of Mound is Tonka Toys. The company began as Mound Metalcraft in 1946 and later became Tonka Toys, Incorporated in 1955. Its signature pressed steel toys made its mark on the toy industry. The setting after the end of World War II proved ideal for the new company. Like its name, the toys garnered a reputation of being indestructible.

During its heyday, the company employed upward of 1,000 employees, mainly women. It manufactured up to 8 million toys a year. Its importance to Mound cannot be overstated. But what made it iconic also set it up for its own end.

In 1991, Hasbro of Pawtucket, Rhode Island purchased the company, leaving a huge void in the city of Mound. However, its legacy lives on with its induction into the National Toy Hall of Fame in 2001. And today, Tonka Toys remain a favorite among toy collectors. Want to know what the fuss is all about? Head over to the Westonka History Museum, #34, to see its collection of vintage toys.

33

Picnic at Surfside Park

Located at the intersection of Bartlett and Commerce Boulevards, Surfside Park is a great place to spend a summer afternoon. Picnic tables and grills set the stage for a delicious outdoor meal. And when you need to cool off, wade in the water at the swimming beach.

The park was formerly known as Mound Bay Park. But thanks to the efforts of local historian Tom Rockvam, the name was changed to reflect its early history as Surfside Park and Beach, dedicated on July 21, 2012.

Did You Know? The shelter located in the park is the old Mound train depot, restored and remodeled.

Bartlett and Commerce Boulevards, Mound

***

The Surfside Story

When you see a park called Surfside, you might wonder if there's a story behind the name. To learn its story is a mini history lesson about the tourist trade in Mound. The story begins with the Chapman House, built in 1876 where Chapman Place Condominiums are located today. The 7-acre resort catered to sportsmen like many of the hotels on the upper lake. The hotel had a fleet of rowboats with guides at the Chapman Boathouse.

Its story follows a familiar theme. A fire engulfed the hotel in 1892. Instead of tossing in the towel, the owners remodeled the hotel, adding a music casino. Back in the day, the Chapman House and Cook's House were the rocking places. During their first summer season, over 1,700 guests visited the hotels. One account of the July 4, 1876 celebration reported that the festivities went on to 3 a.m., until the "*whistle called them for the return voyage.*"

The Chapman House remained open until 1912. When the hotel closed, it became the site of the Glen Isle Casino. The casino was a place for visitors to enjoy rolling skating, billiards, and bowling. It changed hands again, becoming the Surfside Restaurant from 1963 through 1984. The business carried on the Chapman House's tradition of good times until the restaurant was razed in 1986.

Postscript: The history of the Surfside lives on, with the opening of the new, Surfside Bar and Grill, down the road at 2544 Commerce Blvd.

34

Visit the Westonka Historical Society

It's one thing to talk about the history; it's another to experience it. The Westonka Historical Society brings the history of Mound and the surrounding communities alive with exhibits and treasures from the past. Its collection includes the Tonka Toys Collection with over 400 vintage Tonka Toys.

Want to do some research of your own? Be sure and visit the Research Room which includes over 70 history videos. The Westonka Historical Society hosts history talks and other events throughout the year. You can also become a member of the Westonka Historical Society.

Note: A $3 donation is suggested for visiting the site.

5341 Maywood Road, Mound
952-472-9800
westonkahistoricalsociety.org
Saturdays from 10 a.m. to 2 p.m.

***

The Story of the Indian Mounds

One can't talk about Mound without mentioning, well, the mounds. Several accounts exist for the actual number of mounds found on the shores of Lake Minnetonka. A 1881 partnership venture by Alfred Hill and Theodore Lewis tallied almost 7,700 in Minnesota with more than 600 in the Lake Minnetonka area alone.

An 1883 survey put the number at 487. The area along Bluff Lane, for example, had 69 mounds according to the 1883 survey. Some were as large as 50 feet in diameter and 6-foot tall. The survey also identified a similar gathering of mounds on the east side of Seton Channel.

The difference doesn't take into account the number of mounds that might have been pilfered which certainly did occur. And even the 1881 figure might be conservative. An account from an 1875 event included an excavation of a mound. Likely, it wasn't an one-off attraction either.

Newspapers often reported excavations and findings. Residents viewed the mounds as curiosities they could dig up. And many were. Other than opposition from individuals like Peter Gideon, there was little to stop the pillaging. Most disturbing about these stories is that human remains were often found along with the artifacts.

One account exists about County Road 44 in Mound. During construction, a worker lamented how they had to cut through Indian mounds near the shore to finish the job. Another report mentions an Indian mound in Surfside Park that was removed in the 1930s for a barbecue pit. And the mounds weren't confined to Mound. A grading project at the Wayzata Elementary School leveled a mound prior to 1954.

The history of human settlement on Lake Minnetonka begins with Paleo-Indians who migrated to the area around 8000 BC. The so-called Mound Builders followed between 3500 BC and 1500 AD. The occupancy of the area changed when the Mdewakanton people, a subtribe of the Dakota Nation, moved into the region. Lake Minnetonka served as important hunting and fishing grounds as well as sites for collecting maple syrup.

You have to admire any people who could have survived the mosquitoes, the harsh winters, and the hardships of living in these wild places. Remember, before settlement, Minnesota literally was part of the Wild West.

35

Let's Paddle Board!

If you're traveling in Mound, head on down to Bay Rentals and rent a paddle board on Cooks Bay. You can rent one for as little as one hour or the whole day. Learn first hand why it's a great way to work those abs. They also rent out double kayaks and personal watercraft if that's more your speed.

Bay Rentals Inc.
2630 Commerce Blvd, Mound
952-474-0366
bayrentalsmn.com

Or if you're at the other end of town, check out Black Oar Rentals on Spring Park Bay or Tommy's Tonka Trolley in Excelsior.

Did You Know? Black Oar founder, Alex Linnell, was the first person to ever stand-up paddle the entire length of the Mississippi River.

Black Oar Rentals
4012 Shoreline Dr, Spring Park
952-807-2476
theblackoar.com

Tommy's Tonka Trolley
379 Lake Street, Excelsior
952-220-010
tonkatrolley.com

***

Oh, Buoy!

If you're planning to boat on the lake, you have to know what the buoys mean. The buoys on Lake Minnetonka differ slightly from the ones you'll encounter on waters patrolled by the US Coast Guard.

Buoy System

Channel Buoys (Always go between them)
Solid green, lighted green at night
Solid red, lighted red at night (on the right side when upstream)

Point Buoy (Do not pass between the buoy and the shore)
Vertical striped buoy, quick flashing white light

Danger Buoys (Stay away. That's why they're called danger buoys. Do not pass between them.)
White buoy with red top
White buoy with black top

Regulatory Buoys

Orange striped buoy with orange diamond with cross in center—Keep out

Orange striped buoy with orange diamond, no cross—Danger, such as rocks

Orange striped buoy with orange rectangle—Information

Orange striped buoy with orange circle—Controlled area

Mooring Buoys

White balls with blue stripe

Tip: Buoys may be absent at the onset or the end of the season. A depth finder is essentially no matter how well you know the lake. It'll help you find the submerged logs before they find your prop.

36

Party On at the Spirit of the Lakes Festival

There's plenty to do at Mound's grand Spirit of the Lakes Festival, held in July. The festival runs on Friday and Saturday with a whole slate of events. Want to try some local brews? Then, you can't miss the Meet Your Maker! – Minnesota Craft Beverage Fest.

The free event includes an Arts & Crafts Festival at Surfside Park, live music, dancing, and food. You can even enjoy an Al & Alma's Supper Club Charter Cruises for a historic boat tour of Lake Minnetonka. Entertainment includes fun for the kiddies with magic acts and face painting. And to make it easy to take in the festivities, the festival runs a free shuttle bus.

And then there is the Minnesota Wakesurf Championship. Show your stuff at the championship on Cooks Bay in Mound. Part of the Spirit of the Lakes Festival.

spiritofthelakes.com

Minnesota Wakesurf Championship

mnwsc.com

***

Snapshot of the 1890s

- 1890: The Minnetonka Yacht Club's clubhouse opened

- 1890: Arlington House in Wayzata burned down

- 1890: Grain Belt Brewery founder, Frederick Noerenberg, and his family built their estate on the shore of Lake Minnetonka

- 1891: Channel dug separating the two large land masses of Big Island, along with the construction of a foot bridge to Mahpiyata Island

- 1893: Wayzata Depot relocated one mile east of Wayzata at Holdridge as the feud between the village and James Hill catches fire

- 1894: Fire on the west side of Water Street in Excelsior destroys nine buildings

- 1894: Mound City changed its name to Mound

- 1897: The Lafayette Hotel was destroyed by fire

- 1897: Wayzata built its first wooden sidewalks along Lake Street

- 1897: State act established the managed lake level

- 1899: Harrington Inn in Wayzata, said to be the first summer hotel on the lake, burned down

37

Participate in the Running of the Bays Half Marathon

Ready to step up your running game? Then the Running of the Bays Half Marathon is right for you. The certified course starts in Mound and winds through the trails and county roads of the area with a grand finish at the Bethel Methodist Church in Mound.

Not quite ready for a half marathon? The Our Lady of the Lake's Incredible Festival 5k is just your speed. Either way, a run around the lake is a great way to spend a September day.

runningofthebays.com

***

The Cost of a Lake Minnetonka Vacation

- *Day trip*, $2.00: Includes round trip from Wayzata to Excelsior to Cook's Landing or Chapman House, with dinner at Cook's house. You'll get back in time to pick up the afternoon train from Wayzata

- *Day trip*, $0.50: 1901, 1901: round-trip rail ticket to any point on the lake

- *Northland Inn*: 1901-1915. It charged $2 per day for a stay

- *Gleason House*: 1871-1964. $14 a week including meals

- *Upper Lake House*: 1883. single meal, 50 cents

- *Lake Park Hotel*: $2.50 or $3.00 a night, $10 to $15 a week

- *Hotel Lafayette*: $4 a night or about $110 in today's money. Compared to the other hotels, this rate was two or three times that of other accommodations around the lake at the time.

Did You Know? When James Hill purchased the land for the Hotel Lafayette, he paid only $50 an acre or about $1,240 per acre in today's money. Considering that the median house value in 2013 in Minnetonka Beach was $957,558, it's fair to say Hill got a deal.

Hold Hands with Your Babe on the Moonlight Trail Night

The wonderful thing about Lake Minnetonka and the surrounding communities it is that it's just as beautiful and captivating in winter as the summer. And what better way to celebrate it than by taking a luminary-lit trail walk under the glow of a full moon.

A blazing fire pit along the trail will keep you warm and toasty when Jack Frost comes nipping your nose. Music and games add to the fun and enchantment of a winter's eve. Held in the beginning of the year on the full moon. Check out the event's website for upcoming dates.

Dakota Trail
westonkacc.com/moonlight-trail-night

***

"Spend the afternoon. You can't take it with you."
– Annie Dillard

Roll Up for the Mound Magical History Tour

Alas, much of Mound's early history is gone with few remnants remaining. Despite that, you can still experience a bit of Mound's golden age of hotels and summer vacations with a tour of Cooks Bay. This is one thing-to-do that is best by water. You can also walk out on the ice during the winter months when the lake is frozen.

From the center of Cooks Bay looking toward Surfside Park, you are in sight of the locations of three of the iconic hotels of Mound's past. Surfside Park marks the location of the Chapman Hotel and Boathouse. It stood just to the right of the current depot, tucked in the corner.

Turn to the left and south of the depot. This marks the site of the Hotel Buena Vista. If you look to the right of the depot and more toward the center of the beach, you would have seen the Bartlett House.

Now turn around. This is what guests would have seen from the hotels. Beautiful, isn't it? This is one of the many reasons that so many tourists made their way through the Narrows into the upper lake.

Prefer a tour by land? Check out the Historical Tour of the Westonka Area – 2015 available from the Westonka Historical Society. (westonkahistoricalsociety.org)

Note: The areas where the hotels once stood are residences. Please respect their privacy.

Cooks Bay, Mound

***

What's Up With This Upper, Lower, East, South Stuff?

Most of the names of the bays and lakes of Lake Minnetonka recall significant times or people of the past. Then, you come across these lakes: Lower Lake North, Lower Lake South, East Upper Lake, South Upper Lake, and West Upper Lake. What gives? In the days of the hotels, the terminology was more familiar with upper lake hotels distinguishing themselves from the lower lake sites.

The upper/lower distinction speaks to the marked differences that exist between the two divisions, divided by the Narrows. The lower lakes have more open water areas. These are places you're likely to encounter big water. Bigger water means bigger waves. The upper lakes have more islands and smaller bays.

The scenery and natural beauty sets the upper lake apart from the rest. This is one of the reasons why so many advertisements of hotels and attractions on this side of the lake touted its fresh air and health properties.

In fact, the upper lakes were considered a natural wonder. This certainly helped fuel the drive to dredge both the Hull's Narrows and then the Narrows Channel to open these areas to visitors. An advertisement for Cook's House in 1876 called Cooks Bay, "*the most beautiful portion of Lake Minnetonka.*"

What's your favorite bay on the lake and why?

Did You Know? West Upper Lake is the largest of the bays on the lake with about 906 acres, followed by Crystal Bay with about 810 acres.

40

Experience the Incredible at the Our Lady of the Lake's Incredible Festival

Held in September, the Our Lady of the Lake's Incredible Festival is just that—incredible! Three days of fun await. Enjoy live music and an array of foods. Pick up a find at the silent auction. There's a bean bag tournament and bingo to get your game on.

You'll find plenty of things for the kiddies with carnival rides. And you can't have a festival without a beer tent. The festival includes a 5k run with the Running of the Bays Half Marathon. There's something for everyone at the Our Lady of the Lake's Incredible Festival.

2385 Commerce Blvd, Mound
952-472-1284
incrediblefestival.com

***

Wiped Off the Map

The history of the Lake Minnetonka began with three townships: Excelsior, Minnetrista, and Minnetonka. Through the years, they would be divided and subdivided and reshuffled again and again. After the dust cleared, we have our present mix of towns and villages around the lake.

Others exist only in books or as a name of a subdivision or road. Some were annexed into other towns. Yet others failed to incorporate for whatever reason. What follows are a list of some of the towns that once existed, but do not anymore.

Communities That No Longer Exist (but may exist as neighborhoods)
Maplewood
Cottagewood
Minnetonka Mills
Markville
Maplewood
St. Albans
Island City
Tazaska
Minnetonka City
Seton Station
Eureka
Linwood
Chowen
Casco Heights

Did You Know? Author, Blanch Nichols Wilson, described the would-be town of St. Albans as "*of few days and full of trouble,*" in her book, *Minnetonka Story*. The village died out in 1857.

PART VI

Minnetrista

The name, Minnetrista, comes from the Dakota language, meaning crooked water. The name could apply to its other lakes or its shape. Settlers came to the town in 1854 and organized it in 1859.

Minnetrista embodies the past of Lake Minnetonka. It is one of the few towns on the lake with a site on the National Register of Historic Places. Crane Island in West Upper Lake, was home to the Crane Island Association. The association was an island community in the early 1900s. Many of the historic building still exist.

And it's hard to talk about Minnetrista without mentioning the Hermitage. These stories and other await on your visit to this little town.

Did You Know? The Minnetrista area's historical earthquake activity is below the Minnesota state average with a 91 percent smaller chance of a tremor than the overall US average.

41

Find the Peace That Is Halsted Bay

On the southwest side of the lake, the quiet waters of Halsted Bay welcome you. The bay was named after Captain Frank and Major George Halstead, the famous hermit brothers of the lake. Their story follows. The spelling, Halstead, is correct for their surname. It was later changed to its present Halsted spelling for the bay.

Despite its low water quality rating, it still offers charming secluded views especially on its western shores of the 1,700 acres in its watershed. Eagle Bluff towers over the bay on its east side after entering the bay from the channel. The bluffs give way to wetlands as you circle the bay.

Imagine back in the day making the excursion to visit the tranquil home of the Halstead brothers. You're far from the busy lake with its steamers and boats and well before the adjacent Cty. Rd. 44 was constructed in 1905. It's just the calm waters and the dense woods to keep you company. This is a best by boat item.

Did You Know? Boaters launching at Halsted Bay had the highest rate of drain-plug-in-on-arrival violations. Yup, you gotta have it out when the boat is out of the water or pay a hefty fine.

West side of Lake Minnetonka

***

The Hermitage Story

Captain Frank Halstead and his brother, George, are part of the folklore of the upper lake. Like others following dreams of homesteading in Minnesota, Frank Halstead came to the area in 1855 when he built his cabin, calling it the Hermitage. He left the area during the Civil War only to return later to his reclusive lifestyle. Halstead became a well-known curiosity on the lake. Filled with his collection of souvenirs and trinkets, the Hermitage was even a regular stop on lake tours.

People knew Halstead as a hermit. But he hardly fit the Merriam-Webster definition. He seemed nothing like "*one that retires from society and lives in solitude…*" Halstead was active in the community, helping to get the new Narrows Channel dredged. He was the area's first justice of the peace and performed the first marriage. Halstead also started a petition calling for a Mound City school. And he seemed to enjoy his stint as a tourist attraction.

Later in 1876, Frank Halstead built his own lake steamer, the *Mary*, named after his beloved mother. Unfortunately, times were tough for Halstead. His hopes of making money from the *Mary* dwindled. And in June 1876, he vanished only to be found days later, drowned by suicide. But, the legacy of the Hermitage continued.

Major George Halstead, his older brother, had also served with the US Navy during the Civil War. Halstead came to Lake Minnetonka to fulfill his role as executor of his brother's will. He stayed on and, from all appearances, carried on his brother's tradition. Halstead even ran the *Mary* again.

It's important at this point to mention that the *Mary*, like few boats on the lake at the time, had an Ames boiler built by Ames Ironworks. The three-year period between 1877 and 1880 proved deadly for boats with this particular boiler.

First, there was the tragedy of the *Katie May*, launched in the fall of 1876. On June 23, 1887, her boiler exploded, killing three people. At the time, the public viewed it as a tragic accident. But, when the *May Queen* exploded on June 29, 1879, the public took notice. And the *Minneapolis Tribune* expressed outrage, referring to the "*defective boilers or incompetent engineers*" who were endangering tourists. It went so far as to call for a boycott of steamers by would-be travelers to the lake.

But, it wasn't the first time steamers ran afoul of the press. Back in 1871, the *St. Paul Pioneer Press* started its own campaign against the "*murderous*" steamers and alleging that condemned boats were still on the water. In the summer of 1880, events again took a tragic turn.

You can well imagine the furor when on July 1, 1880, the *Mary* suffered a similar fate and exploded, killing three people. Writers for the *Minneapolis Tribune* were more enraged and directed their ire now at the state government. One editorial asked, "*How long will the legislature of Minnesota remain insensible to the dangers upon the small lakes of the state?"* In a reference to the three explosions, another Minneapolis paper referred to them as *"The Minnetonka Murderers."* At this time, there were not laws compelling boat owners to test their boilers for safe, hence, the outcry.

At the time, public opinion waged its own war against George Halstead, likening his actions to that of murder. He managed to weather the storm and continued on at the Hermitage as one of the lake's tourist attractions. But fate still had yet one more card to play in what some may have called karma.

On September 6, 1901, the Hermitage started on fire, killing Halstead. Curiously, the fire didn't stop the tourists, who still came to this part of the lake to view the site. Though long gone, the legend of the two brothers continues. And if rumors are still to be believed, they rest in peace on the land they loved in unmarked graves. Some have even suggested that ghosts of the brothers still roam the shoreline.

Did You Know? After George Halstead died, the Hermitage was sold. A condition of sale to C.M. Loring of the Pillsbury Flour Mill Company was the preservation of the graves of the Halstead brothers. The land became the Woodend Dairy Farm.

42

Learn the Meaning of Community at Crane Island

Located in West Upper Lake, Crane Island is a bit of a misnomer, referring to a different type of bird all together. The island was named for the great number of herons and cormorants that once nested here. Residents revered the birds with a penalty for shooting them. Today, federal law protects these birds.

Though not cranes, herons are interesting birds. Their slow gait is almost comical as they wade through shallow waters on the lookout for fish, scraps, nestlings, and small mammals. They won't turn down the occasional frog either.

They nest communally in areas called rookeries. It is not unusual for up to be upward of 500 nests at a site. Herons have a loyalty to a rookery, coming back to nest year-after-year. That habit certainly made the name stick with the early settlers.

The 9.6-acre Crane Island offered a perfect location. Being relatively remote, it offered an important attraction for a bird that can be very flighty around humans. Other than the occasional bald eagle, they were safe here.

Their communal nesting also has its consequences. As it often happens, the concentration of guano on the trees ends up killing them or at least weakening them to the point that they become vulnerable to high winds. The rookery didn't last long. When it did succumb to the elements, it opened the door for human settlement of the island.

Today, Crane Island is part of the National Register of Historic Places. It became home to the Crane Island Association, whose story follows. Interestingly, the association followed in the footsteps of the herons, creating their own colony.

Eighteen cottages exist on the island including the caretaker's cabin in the center and 23 outbuildings. Of the cottages, 13 were built prior to 1915. Plantings by residents of the island provided privacy, and thus, the concealment of some of the cottages today.

As you can well imagine, Crane Island and its intact cottages and outbuildings are unique in many respects. The National Park Service thought so too. On August 5, 1991, Crane Island entered the National Register of Historic Places.

Note: Crane Island is privately owned. Docking on the island is prohibited. Best by water.

Did You Know? The area north of Crane Island is good for northern pike and bass fishing. Oh, and by the way, the only crane seen in the Lake Minnetonka area is the sandhill crane—and it's not even in the same family as herons.

Location: West Upper Lake, Minnetrista

***

The Crane Island Association

The Crane Island Association holds a unique place in history of Lake Minnetonka. First, let's put it in context. Before 1873, travel between the upper and lower lakes was a arduous undertaking. The channel between the two was inadequate for navigation by bigger boats. That all changed with the dredging of Hull's Narrows via the Old Channel Bay in 1873. It ushered in an era of change.

Smaller hotels turned into luxury accommodations as the tourist trade took off. During the 1883 summer season, over 10,000 guests stayed at the three grand hotels alone. The influx of tourists underscored the different values of the people who lived on the lake. But as quickly as it rose, the tourist industry declined until only six hotels remained after the end of World War I.

From seasonal cottagers to local communities, the Lake Minnetonka area continued to evolve. It was the vision of Charles E. Woodward to create a community of people of like-minded people on the upper lake. Two such communities existed on the lake then, the Baptist Assembly Grounds near Mound and the Methodist Groveland Young People's Assembly on Wayzata Bay. The Crane Island Association differed with its private ownership of the lots and structures on them.

Crane Island was surveyed and divided into 26 lots, each with 100 foot of shoreline and 200 feet deep. Then, on June 14, 1906, the association was incorporated. Landowners cleared the island, creating a commons area and a caretaker's cabin. By 1915, the community was established. The electric streetcar line served islanders with streetcar boats ferrying them to and fro.

The mission of the association was to provide "… *summer homes away from the noise and confusion of the city* …" Thus, members practiced temperance and limited Sunday activities. Each cottage posted the rules of the association for residents and guests to the island with an expectation that all would adhere to them. And so the Crane Island Association continued, a well-preserved example of a community of individuals with a common cause.

43

Enjoy the Outdoors at the Lake Minnetonka Regional Park

Lake Minnetonka Regional Park offers a variety of recreational activities sure to please. A sand-bottom swimming pond is open until sunset daily. Looking to be a landlubber today? There are hiking trails, a 3-hole disc golf practice area, fishing pier, and a children's play area. The park is dog friendly, with a dog trail. And for a bit of history, check out the Schmid house.

Joseph and Benedict Schmid were German immigrants who came to the area in the 1850s. They built the farmhouse in 1876. With the rising tourist trade, the brothers began to sell off their property in 1901. They abandoned the farmhouse which continued to be occupied by tenant farmers through 1950.

Did You Know? The Three Rivers Park District is seeking nomination for the Schmid farmhouse to be placed on the National Register of Historic Places.

4610 County Road 44, Minnetrista

***

The Story of Charles May

When you talk about Lake Minnetonka's steamboat history, you have to include Charles May. May is credited for creating the first fleet of steamboats on the lake in 1874. He also ran a barrel stave company. The steamer venture was a means to haul his production to Wayzata.

He acquired several boats during his tenure, including the 65-foot propeller *May Queen*, the sidewheeler *Rambler*, the propellers *Kate/Katie May/Saucy Kate*, *City of Minneapolis*, and *Mary/Hiawatha/Scandinavian/Star*. (The / between names indicates a change of name, often following a restoration or resale.)

May dappled in other ventures too. For a while, he tried hauling wheat. And for a time, he ran a small hotel near St. Albans. But his legacy with the steamers earned him a place in history, or infamy as some may say. The troubles began on June 23, 1877 when the *Katie May* exploded, killing three people. If that weren't enough the *May Queen* suffered a similar fate in 1879. Fortunately, no one was killed, but it put the spotlight on his fleet of steamers.

Some steamers were recovered and rebuilt. Others like the *Saucy Kate* didn't fare as lucky, having been burned off of Solberg's Point. But the trouble with steamers wasn't over yet. In 1880, yet another steamer, the *Mary* owned by George Halstead, exploded, taking three lives with her. He got out of the steamer business, selling his fleet to the Lake Minnetonka Navigation Company.

But leave it to May to feel the itch again. He built the *W.D. Washburn* with a double propeller shaft. She probably was a handful. This was evident when she crashed into the Excelsior Docks, causing extensive damage. After this fiasco, May sold the *W.D. Washburn*.

PART VII

Shorewood

Not all towns around Lake Minnetonka are large. This six-mile long town was part of the former Excelsior Township. A town doesn't have to be big to have a significant place in history.

Shorewood's claim-to-fame is one of its most famous residents, Peter Gideon. Gideon realized his calling early in life. After settling in Minnesota, he became a prominent figure in horticulture, developing the winter-hardy Wealthy apple. You can't exaggerate his contributions to the trade with a beautiful bay that bears his name.

44

Experience the Big Woods at Gideon Glen

At the intersection of Smithtown Road and County Road 19, the 5.8-acre Gideon Glen Wetland Restoration/Water Quality Demonstration Project is a project of the Minnehaha Creek Watershed District (MCWD). Its purpose is to build understanding and appreciation for the area's unique natural environment.

A short stone path winds through wetlands with interpretative signs to guide your way. Surface runoff goes through four stages of algae and pollution removal on its way to Lake Minnetonka. The site offers another educational opportunity of a different sort.

See the landscape as it once was. Gideon Glen includes a restored black ash swamp and a remnant of the Big Woods, like what you would have seen before Lake Minnetonka was settled.

The old growth forest has maple and basswood trees over 150 years old, which escaped the lumberjack's ax and sawmills. The MCWD estimates that 98 percent of the original Big Woods is gone, making places like Gideon Glen very special and worth the stop.

Intersection of Smithtown Road and County Road 19
Shorewood, MN
City of Shorewood: 952-474-3236

***

The Farms of Lake Minnetonka

Besides tourism, Lake Minnetonka was once known for its farms. James Hill had his own 160-acre farm, appropriately called, the Hillier, or Crystal Bay Farm by locals. It was a fleeting venture, lasting only until 1883 when Hill moved on to bigger enterprises in the environs around St. Paul.

Farms came in all sizes including the 1,000-acre Woodend Farm in Minnetrista which produced Holsteins and Guernseys. Wayzata's own dairy industry was a $2 million one back in 1930. And the farms were not of a peasant nature. Rather, they were "*gentleman's farms.*"

The 111-acre Highcroft estate included a dairy farm—along with its 30-room mansion and 40 by 60 foot great hall. Shorewood also had its own large farm, the 800-acre Boulder Bridge Farm near Smithtown Bay. Like Woodend, the farm raised Guernseys along with Belgian horses.

As you probably can guess, land values won out. The owners sold the farms. They were subdivided. The only remnant of many of the old ones is a name of a subdivision. But not all farms suffered the same fate. The Summit Park Farm in Wayzata is now the Wayzata Country Club. And the Lafayette Hotel is in part, Minnetonka Beach and the Lafayette Club, the latter a nod to the Hotel Lafayette.

45

Visit the to Peter Gideon Monument

It's only fitting that Shorewood and the Lake Minnetonka pay tribute to the man who gave us the Wealthy apple. He brought the practice of producing winter-hardy produce to Lake Minnetonka. The story of Peter Gideon's discovery follows. The land you see is only part of the estate where he began his horticulture experiments of the man who would become, "*the father of fruit breeding in the Midwest.*" The memorial was dedicated on June 16, 1912.

The National Park Service designated the Gideon Homestead and land as part of the National Register of Historic Places in 1974. Some of his original apples planted between 1854 and 1899 still thrived then. In fact, the original apple tree was located less than 500 yards from the monument. Peter Gideon was also known to be a fierce protector of Indian mounds which existed on his property.

Gideons Bay is located just west out of Excelsior Bay, northeast of the monument. The towns of Excelsior, Shorewood and Tonka Bay circle its shores. One look, and you'll find out why it's an A-graded bay in more ways than one.

Note: While you can view the monument, Glen Road is a residential area, with some private roads. Please respect their privacy.

Cty Rte. 19 and Glen Road (pull off the side of the road to view), Shorewood

***

Peter Gideon and the Wealthy Apple

Peter Gideon and his wife, Wealthy Gideon nee' Hull, came to the Lake Minnetonka area in the fall of 1853. Wealthy was the daughter of Reverend Stephen Hull of Hull's Narrows fame (#20).

Gideon claimed his 160 acres near Gideons Bay. Not unlike Minnesota wine growers today with grapes, his aim was to develop an apple that could survive the Minnesota winters. Gardeners can appreciate the challenges of growing plants in USDA Plant Hardiness Zones 4 and 5. This means winters with extreme cold temperatures of –10 to –25 degrees Fahrenheit.

You could say that Peter Gideon had fruit growing in his blood. He had a lifelong interest in growing things even as a child. But producing a winter-hardy variety proved to be a challenge. Gideon's Wealthy apple took years to develop. Like Minnesota snowbirds, apples typically prefer warmer climes.

But Gideon succeeded in 1868, making it the first apple cultivar to withstand the Minnesota winters after 10 years and 350 trees. Gideon's Wealthy apple is a tart, juicy fruit that matures in

September, making it one of the earlier harvested varieties. It's a good choice for backyard orchardists today because of its long bloom period and great pollinating potential for other apple trees. He produced other varieties, including his Peter and Gideon apples.

In 1878, he became the first superintendent of the 116-acre state experimental fruit farm until 1889. Though he passed away in 1899, his Wealthy apple became one of the five leading apples grown in the United States by the 1900s. In *Tales of Tonka*, author, Ellen Wilson Meyer, described the Wealthy apple as *"the best apple discovered since Adam and Eve left the Garden of Eden."*

Peter Gideon's legacy lives on with the fruits of Wealthy apple living on with other apples, such as the Haralson and with the backyard orchardists who prize its strawberry-like taste.

Speaking of Haralson, Charles Haralson was a resident of Deephaven. As the name suggests, he developed Minnesota-ready fruits too, including his signature Haralson apple available in 1923. He also developed other varieties, including the Minnehaha and Wedge apples as well as winter-hardy raspberries, currants, plums, and his own, Deephaven strawberry.

The quest for winter-hardy fruits went beyond apples. Horticulturists pursued similar ventures, including raspberries and other fruits. Another notable individual was German-born, Wendelin Grimm who developed his winter-hardy Grimm's alfalfa for livestock feed.

PART VIII

Tonka Bay

Like Spring Park, Tonka Bay owed some of its early popularity to a grand hotel. The Minnetonka Bay Hotel/Lake Park Hotel/Tonka Bay Hotel was a dominant feature from 1879 to 1913. But Tonka Bay's place in history goes back further.

Stephen Hull, an early Tonka Bay settler, settled near the first channel to separate the upper and lower lakes. Before the channel known as Hull's Narrows opened, the lakes were all but separated. Boat traffic was only possible with smaller crafts. The dredging of the larger Narrows Channel opened up steamboat traffic between the lakes.

Tourism to the upper lake soon followed. Tonka Bay was incorporated as a village on September 11, 1901. Today, it carries on as a small but mighty village on the lake.

46

Catch Some Rays at Tonka Bay's Crescent Public Beach

Crescent Beach is jointly owned and operated by the cities of Tonka Bay and Shorewood. It offers a unique view of East Upper Lake. Take in the sights of the big waters of Lake Minnetonka. Life guards are on duty from 12 p.m. to 5 p.m., from June through August. But don't limit yourself to the beach. The city of Shorewood has six parks of its own with about 100 acres dedicated to fun and enjoyment.

Note: Alcohol and glass containers are not permitted.

240 Birch Bluff Road, Tonka Bay
Information: 952-474-7994

***

The Tonka Bay Hotel (1879-1913)

You can't talk about Tonka Bay without mentioning the Tonka Bay Hotel. The Tonka Bay Hotel began its short run in 1879 as the Minnetonka Park Hotel, then the Lake Park Hotel, and later renamed to the Tonka Bay Hotel. This grand hotel could accommodate 1,000 guests and seat over 400 in its opulent dining room on its 250-acre site with almost five miles of shoreline.

On the "*boot*" jutting into Lower Lake South, its attractions included a 420-foot porch, rolling rink, tennis courts, horse stables, and a casino. It had verandas on all sides and all floors. The latter became part of its brand, if you will, with its slogan, "*Every room on a veranda.*"

The hotel sat west of the present-day Tonka Bay Marina. Fink's Pavilion was on the marina's east side. The pavilion advertised "*If you don't enjoy yourself here, it is your own fault,*" saying that there was "… *no better bathing beach in Minnesota.*"

You could reach the hotel by taking one of the six trains daily that stopped at the nearby depot and take a short two minute walk to hotel. And remember these were the days before Samsonite bags with rollers.

The Tonka Bay Hotel boasted modern amenities including 16 electric lights and a telephone. Its boathouse had fleets of row and sail boats. There was a soda fountain and confectionery counter. There was also an extensive news stand at the hotel.

The health benefits of the good lake air were widely touted then. And the Lake Park Hotel/Tonka Bay Hotel joined this cause as part of the Chautauqua assembly lecture circuit. And unlike James Hill and his defiance against liquor laws, the Lake Park Hotel/Tonka Bay Hotel did not serve or permit alcohol.

Before the Hotel Lafayette opened in 1882, the Tonka Bay Hotel was the largest of the grand hotels on the lake. But like other luxury hotels, the Tonka Bay Hotel's time was short-lived. It closed in 1911. The public salvaged the hotel's leftover bits and pieces before the hotel was razed in 1913.

47

Relive the Early Days of Steamers at the Old Channel Bay

The original channel, Hull's Narrows, was the only navigable way get from the upper and lower lakes. The channel was a 40-acre marshy area of wild rice. It had been a small creek widened and deepened to form a channel.

Even calling it a channel was a stretch. Dredged in 1873, the depth of the channel varied from three to five feet. Its width varied as well from 25 to 50 feet. The present-day view gives you a good idea of the difficulty traveling between the upper and lower lakes.

To make matters worse, it wasn't the nice straight channel it is now at the Narrows Channel. Rather, the old channel meandered on its path between lower and upper lakes. You can imagine how difficult it was to navigate. And then, you had the strong currents, droughts, and the dam at Minnetonka Mills to say nothing of the boat traffic itself, all adding to the troubles.

The situation begged for a resolution. Straightening and dredging the channel were the first order of business, as per recommendations by civil engineer and Spring Park resident, George W. Cooley. Today, you can see the old channel from the road or by boat. But these are shallow waters. Small boats only. For the rest of the story, go the Orono Section, Narrows Channel, #20.

Did You Know? During World War II, the military considered Lake Minnetonka a possible enemy target. The US Coast Guard swept the lake for hidden mines. On October 14, 1942, the area experienced its first air raid drill between 9:30 p.m. and 10 p.m. Following protocol, all electricity was turned off during the drill.

Location: Old Channel Bay on Manitou Road, Tonka Bay

***

Boat Names Sure to Raise an Eyebrow

Some scoff at the idea of naming a boat, saying they prefers anonymity. And that's probably not a bad idea. But you have to laugh when you see some of the boat names on the lake. And in the interests of anonymity, what follows are fun names, all made up. If they exist on the lake, I haven't spotted them.

- *Martini Cruiser*

- *It's Five O'Clock Somewhere*

- *Over the Limit*

- *Over Board*

- *On for the Road*

- *The Blind Pig*

- *Boozer*
- *Penalty Box*
- *Drunken Goat*
- *Loaded Llama*
- *Tipsy Turtle*
- *Tanked Trout*
- *BUD Y ZER*
- *Pickled Perch*
- *Anita Cocktail*

48

Get the Fever, the Arctic Fever

What do Minnesotans do when the weather gets cold? We celebrate the winter! And that's what the Arctic Fever is all about. Sponsored by the cities of Tonka Bay, Shorewood, and Excelsior, the weekend event includes a host of activities sure to please everyone. Try your hand at a snow sculpture. How about some icefishing? Or maybe a fat bike race is more your speed.

Have you ever wanted to ride in a dog sled or take a sleigh ride? Here's your chance. When you get done, you can warm up at a bonfire and enjoy some tasty s'mores. And it wouldn't be a proper festival without a brew party, courtesy of Excelsior Brew. Don't let winter get you down. Get the fever!

Did You Know? When the infamous Wets versus Drys battles ensued, Tonka Bay was the last holdout. The entire lake went over to the dark side in 1915.

arcticfever.net

***

Galpin Lake

One of the early settlers to Lake Minnetonka was Reverend Charles Galpin who founded the Independent Church of Excelsior in 1853. Reverend Galpin influenced the area in many ways. For a time, he operated the first steamboat on the lake, the *Governor Ramsey*. He even delivered mail on the lake and shuttled travelers to and fro. Galpin ran Excelsior's first hotel, the Galpin House which opened in 1854.

Galpin also influenced education, a mission that ranked high for many settlers. He founded the Excelsior Institute in 1857 and the Excelsior Academy in 1885. Galpin was a man of many skills as a dentist, tin smith, and Latin scholar. History remembers him with the Galpin Lake, a separate body of water located south of Highway 7 off of Mill Street. Like many of Excelsior's founders, he is buried in Oak Hill Cemetery.

PART IX

Excelsior

The name, Excelsior, comes from the Henry Wadsworth Longfellow poem of the same name. It means ever upward, or if you prefer the Latin phrase, *Scopus meus excelsior est* ("my goal is higher"). One of the early settlers was George Betram of New York.

Betram did what many visitors still do today. When he visited the area, he fell in love with the lake. He returned to New York and founded the Excelsior Pioneer Association. These early settlers made Excelsior the first community on Lake Minnetonka.

Excelsior embraced tourism. While Wayzata had the railroad, Excelsior had the hotels. It had more boarding houses and hotels than any other village on the lake. But one of its early claims to fame was its role as the most prominent dry town. Wayzata traded jabs with James Hill. Excelsior had its battles with the so-called Wets and Drys.

Today, Excelsior remains a tourist destination. Charter boats including the *Minnehaha* keep the tradition alive. And the town keeps welcoming visitors again and again.

49

Imagine an Island Paradise at Gale Island

Once called Gooseberry Island, Harlow Gale purchased Gale Island around 1860 for under a reported $4, a steal at any time. And imagine living on your own island paradise. In 1873, Gale built a home on the island. It was the first summer residence on Lake Minnetonka.

When Harlow Gale passed away, the Tryon family moved to the island each June. As the late Isabel Tryon Thibault recalled, "... *our life revolved around boats*," as recorded in the *Tales of Tonka*. And why wouldn't it?

With its location in the big waters of Lower Lake South, you'd think that it would be windy on the island. Isabel and her sister, Mary, loved the island even with its wind and spray. And could you imagine stargazing or watching meteor showers on a moonless night? Priceless!

Note: The entire island is privately owned. Best viewed by water.

Did You Know? Author, Elizabeth Fries Ellet, gave her own name to Gale Island, calling it Ellet Island. She named other places on the lake, often after her favorite writers.

Location: Lower Lake South

***

Former Names

One thing becomes apparent when delving into the history of Lake Minnetonka: things change. Buildings and houses get moved or razed. Even the hills are not permanent. And so it is with the names of landmarks. The reasons vary. Owners, past and present, lend their name to a place. Sometimes an event, real or not, gives a landmark a character all its own. The Dakota influence, of course, is evident everywhere from the names of bays and towns to the lake itself.

During the course of my research, I came across a myriad of former names. While some may be obvious, other former names leave you wondering about the story behind the name. And trust me; there's always a story. The list below contains the *present name*, followed by other names it has been known as through its history.

- *Arcola*: Northwood
- *Big Island*: Cottage Island, Owens Island, Meeker Island, Morse Island
- *Bracketts Point*: Starvation Point, Orono Point
- *Breezy Point*: Spirit Knob
- *Bug Island*: Tahtu Island
- *Carsons Bay*: Pig Inlet

- *Casco Point*: Spring Park Point

- *Country Road #15*: County Road #7

- *Deephaven*: Northome

- *Gale Island*: Gooseberry Island, Bright Woods, Groves Island, Ellet Island

- *Grays Bay*: Lake Browning

- *Highway 7*: Yellowstone Trail

- *Lafayette Bay*: Holmes Bay

- *Lafayette Club*: Minnetonka Pleasure Club

- *Lake Minnetonka*: Peninsula Lake

- *Long Lake*: Tamarack

- *Lookout Point*: Blithwood, Harrington's Point

- *Minnehaha Creek*: Little River, Brown's River

- *Minnetonka Beach*: Island City

- *Minnetrista*: German Home

- *Mound*: Mound City

- *Navarre*: Jackson's Corner (Railway Stop: Langdon)

- *Phelps Island*: Noble Island, North Shore Park

- *Shady Island*: Rockwell Island

- *Shaver Park*: Hoagland Woods

- *Spray Island*: Hog Island

- *Spring Park Bay*: Byer's Bay

- *Tanager Lake*: Mud Lake

- *The Narrows*: Hull's Narrows
- *Wawatasso Island*: Dunlap's Island, Fire-fly Island
- *Wayzata*: Wayzata City, Freeport
- *Wayzata Bay*: Lake Bryant

50

Reflect on Life at the Trinity Episcopal Church

The Trinity Episcopal Church began its story with the first settlers to the area in the 1850s. Their first church was a log church on St. Albans Bay. This church is the second building for the parish. Completed in 1863, the formed concrete construction used lake shore stones and Shakopee lime to give its characteristic color and design, making it a true Minnetonka icon.

The church originally was located on Third Street from 1863 to 1907. It was moved to its present location with the construction of the street car trolley line in 1907. The federal government declared the church a National Historic Monument in 1933.

Since that time, the church has seen several renovations. You can still see its original structure. You might also notice how small it originally was compared to its present size. It is one of the few examples of early construction on the lake.

Did You Know? The Trinity Episcopal Church was the first building in the Lake Minnetonka area exclusively for church services.

Trinity Episcopal Church
322 Second Street, Excelsior

***

Snapshot of the 1900s

- 1900: Railroad comes to Mound

- 1901: George C. Andrews and George B. Dayton open the Northland Inn, Wayzata

- 1902: Telephone service comes to Mound

- 1904: First speed limit signs in Wayzata for 8 mph within village limits

- 1904: Maplewood Inn in Deephaven was destroyed by fire

- 1904: Twin City Rapid Transit Company started streetcar line to Excelsior

- 1904: Excelsior Casino opens

- 1906: Big Island Amusement Park opens

- 1906: Feud between James Hill and the village of Wayzata reaches a compromise with the return of the depot to the town

- 1907: Hotel St. Louis demolished

- 1908: Last wolf bounty paid in Lake Minnetonka area

- 1909: The 125-foot steamboat, *Excelsior*, was burned as part of tourist spectacle, attracting some 5,000 onlookers

Travel on the Road to Wellness at St. Albans Bay

#51: St. Albans Bay

St. Albans Bay sits east of Excelsior Bay. Like other landmarks across Lake Minnetonka, the bay shares a name with a place back East. Enos Day of St. Albans, Vermont, named the bay after reaching Excelsior in 1856. While not technically quiet waters, you'll get that experience in this bay.

Unlike many bays, St. Albans Bay has extensive No Wake/Slow Wake zones. In a way, it hearkens back to its past as a place for relaxation. Author, Blanche Nichols Wilson, described St. Albans Bay as "*one of Nature's perfect poems*" in her book, *Minnetonka Story*.

The bay's claim to fame comes from its legendary St. Albans Bay Hotel and Health Resort. Don't let the resort bit fool you. It operated as a sanitarium for recuperation and convalescence from illness. The fresh air and the views of Lake Minnetonka certainly helped that cause .

After a fire in 1914, the resort re-branded itself. It became the St. Albans Keepwell Resort. It had modern amenities such as a bathing beach, tennis courts, and bowling alleys to lead you on the road to wellness. With its 2,000-foot shoreline, it had much to offer for a relaxing stay.

Did You Know? A plan for the village of St. Albans was filed in 1853 that would have created a town that would have extended to southern Deephaven's west border.

Location: Accessible from Excelsior Bay under the St. Albans bridge

***

The Steamboat Graveyard

Many parts of Lake Minnetonka have the unfortunate association as a steamboat graveyard. When shrinking revenues made having a boat too expensive, it wasn't unusual to see them end up on the bottom of the lake. St. Albans Bay shared this same legacy. A 2012 survey by Maritime Heritage Minnesota identified seven anomalies in St. Albans Bay alone.

One of its most famous wrecks is the *Belle of Minnetonka*, which was scuttled and sunk here in 1892. All that remains of her now is a 72-foot wreck site. Another wreck located in the bay may be one of Captain John Johnson's dredges. The organization considers this wreck to be high priority because it represents a new vessel type found in Lake Minnetonka.

One of the more infamous of scuttled crafts are the remains of the excursion boat, the *Excelsior*. The Big Island Amusement Park decided to burn the *Excelsior* in a last-ditch effort to raise revenue. But it wasn't a small campfire with a wienie roast. When she was on the water, the *Excelsior* was a 125-foot steamer with a 800-passenger capacity. It even had its own restaurant.

But on August 12, 1909 at 9 p.m., she became a *"ship on fire at sea."* The event became a tourist attraction, bringing thousands of visitors to witness the inferno. Today, like many boats purposely scuttled, she remains at the bottom of the lake near Big Island.

52

Cruise the Lake on the Historic Minnehaha

The Museum of Lake Minnetonka offers standard cruises on the *Minnehaha* on weekends and holidays starting Memorial Day weekend. The Grand Wayzata excursions include a short layover in Wayzata. It also offers specialty cruises on Wednesday and Thursday evenings. You can purchase tickets on the boats, but be aware that these trips are very popular. And like the streetcars, the *Minnehaha* is not handicap accessible.

You can even make it an all-day event with Wayzata Concert Series cruises, fall color tours, and local event cruises. Or if you really want to wow your friends and family, charter the *Minnehaha* for your own event. Call for more information.

The Twin City Rapid Transit Company operated streetcar boats from 1906 to 1926. Six streetcar boats traveled the lake to 27 different stops. They included several familiar names, including *Como, Harriet, Hopkins, Minnehaha, Stillwater*, and *White Bear*. The streetcar boats also transported commuters

For 10 cents, up to 130 passengers could travel between two points. As anyone who travels around the lake will tell you, sometimes it's quicker and easier to go by boat. Back in the day, even department stores like Dayton's delivered goods by water.

But alas, with the rise of automobiles came the demise of the streetcar boats in 1926. Three out of the six boats were scuttled off of Big Island, including the *Minnehaha*. The others were scrapped, with the *Hopkins* going into private hands until it too suffered the same fate. The *Minnehaha* was recovered in 1980 and again on the water after restoration in 1996.

Note: Food and alcohol are not permitted on the boat.

Did You Know? While some may think that Minnehaha is a short joke, it is the name of a fictional American Indian woman from Henry Wadsworth Longfellow's 1855 poem, *The Song of Hiawatha*. Several meanings exist for the name, including laughing water.

400 Lake Street, Excelsior
952-474-2115 (messages only)
steamboatminnehaha.org

Wayzata dock: 402 E Lake Street, Wayzata (in front of the Depot)

***

Oh, the Things You Find at the Bottom of a Lake

Findings from a 2012 survey report by Maritime Heritage Minnesota

- Boats of all kinds, including steamers, tugboats, streetcar boats, barges, pontoon boats
- Dredges
- Big Island pier, arch bases
- Chairs
- Diving tower
- Several possible piers
- Pilings
- Fish house

Several bays are the watery graves of wrecks and other lost structures including Crystal, Smiths, Browns, Wayzata, Grays, Robinsons, Lafayette, Carsons, and Gideons Bays. Both Lower Lake North and South contain various anomalies and possible wrecks.

Another source of objects at the bottom of the lake comes from an accepted practice of the day. When the lake was iced over, some would haul pallets of trash by horse onto the surface. When the ice began to melt...

53

Pretend It's 1906 at the Big Island Amusement Park

During the early 1900s, the Twin City Rapid Transit (TCRT) expanded its presence on the Lake Minnetonka. The crowning touch was the 65-acre Big Island Amusement Park opened on August 5, 1906. This was the TCRT's second venture into the amusement park business, with the first being the Wildwood Amusement Park at White Bear Lake.

Like the Wildwood, there was concern that another amusement park would bring saloons and their associated woes to Lake Minnetonka. Despite these local reservations, the TCRT went ahead with the park. Imagine this scenario for an outing.

It's summer. You take a streetcar boat to Big Island. The park's 200-foot Electric Tower attracted your attention the last time you were on the lake. Its dazzling display lit up the lake. Now you're here.

Where to begin? You could go the amusement park and ride a roller coaster. Or perhaps you might take a leisurely spin on the carousel. Maybe you want to walk around and enjoy the aviary or the aquarium. Looking for something more active?

How about some music at the 15,000-seat music casino or the dance pavilion? When you've had your fill of dancing, you could stroll the grounds, maybe topping it off with a picnic like thousands of others did when visiting the park. Sounds like a great afternoon, doesn't it?

The Big Island Amusement Park's run was short, even tragically short given its many attractions. It stayed open for only six summer seasons before shutting down in 1911. Its carousel went to Valleyfair. But, contrary to popular belief, the roller coaster did not make the cut. Instead, it was dismantled and demolished.

Metal and structures retrieved from the once-flourishing park would serve the war effort during WWI. The tower was melted, and other bits salvaged or scraped. While the park may have closed, another chapter to the island's story would soon begin.

The history of Big Island then took a curious turn. In 1915, it became the site for a game farm for raising prairie chickens. When that didn't pan out, the farm raised pheasants instead. This venture took off. Within nine years, there was a hunting season for the upland game. The game farm soon outgrew the island. It was moved to upper lake in Mound.

Big Island would continue to play a role in the Lake Minnetonka community. In 1923, it once again served the war effort becoming the Big Island Veterans Camp. Later, the city of Orono would purchase a 56-acre parcel on the eastern side of the island in 2006.

A conservation easement covers the majority of the former Veterans Camp. Today, the city of Orono and the Minnehaha Creek Watershed District jointly manage the Big Island Nature Park.

Alcohol, glass containers, and open fires are prohibited. Sorry, overnight camping is not allowed. Leashed pets are welcome. While you can visit the park, other areas on Big Island are private. Please follow park rules and honor boundaries. The Sheriff's Water Patrol keeps an eye on the park.

Tip: A good way to see the sites of the Big Island Amusement Park is by geocaching. Many geocaches identify specific areas on the island.

Did You Know? Journalist, A.S. Dimond named Big Island in the *Lake Minnetonka Tourist* in 1876. It had been known off and on as Morse Island/Big Island. Then, after about 1906, it became known simply as Big Island.

Lower Lake South

***

The Islands – Part 1

While an island might seem like an island, various classification criteria mean that the actual number may vary depending upon your source. Technically, it is a body of land surrounded by water. By that definition, there are numerous clearly defined islands. However, Lake Minnetonka also has many sites that may not be islands in the strict sense.

In fact, numerous unnamed islands exist around the lake, connected to the shore by sandbars and therefore, not truly surrounded by water. The following list includes the well-known islands, natural and man made, with a brief explanation of each. Like a lot of landmarks and place names, a few of the islands make you wonder about the story behind the name. For my part, Bug Island can remain a mystery.

Big Island (Lower Lake South)
See history of Big Island on #19 in the Orono section

Bug Island (St. Louis Bay)
Formerly Tahtu Island, it became the site for the Minnetonka Ice Yacht clubhouse. The name, Tahtu, comes from Charles Gibson who named it after his boat.

Crane Island (West Upper Lake)
See Crane Island, #42, in the Minnetrista section

Deering Island (West Arm)
Once owned by Charles W. Deering in the 1880s, it was the home base for his steamer, the *Florence M. Deering*. Deering led excursions on the lake. He and his family lived on the island five months out of the year.

Eagle Island (West Upper Lake)
Named for the eagles that once nested there regularly

Enchanted Island (Phelps Bay)
Legend has it that it was considered a sacred place, the name given by settlers in the pre-settlement days. Commodore Zimmerman purchased the island in 1877 from the Sioux City Railway. He built a cottage here which later became Boulder Lodge.

54

Ride the Rail at Haskell's Port of Excelsior

The unassuming appearance of this watering hole belies its place as a celebrated local hangout. And once the wait staff learn your beverage of choice, you can count yourself among the ranks of the regulars. But Haskell's is more than friendly service and great burgers. It also offers some of the best people-watching around outside on the rail. Grab a seat on the patio and see why parallel-parking makes a hilarious spectator sport!

Tip: You can boat to Haskell's and dock at the Excelsior Docks. If you boat, bring quarters to feed the parking meters.

Did You Know? Excelsior was also known as Vineyards for the fine grapes produced in the area.

1 Water Street, Excelsior
952-474-0937
haskellsport.com

***

The White House and the Missing Hills

Way before Haskell's became Haskell's, the corner of Water and Lake Streets looked different. Anderson Jenkins of Indiana was the first resident of No. 1 Water Street. Jenkins lived a sad life, having previously lost his first two wives to tuberculosis.

He found happiness with his third wife in the yellow cottage he built on this spot. His son took over the house when Anderson passed, converting the home into a boarding house. He was named it the White House for its white exterior color.

The house changed ownership and names a few times before the Women's Club of Minnetonka bought it. The group then, in turn, donated the house to the Minnesota Sunshine Society. Then, it became a home for the aged.

The home lasted until 1946 when it was demolished. But, wait, there's more! It wasn't just the house that got carried away. The White House once stood on a hill overlooking Lake Minnetonka. When the building went, so did the hill.

55

Get Nostalgic at the Excelsior Amusement Park

Lake Minnetonka had a love affair with amusement parks. After the Big Island Amusement Park closed, Excelsior got into the game again in 1925. The Excelsior Amusement Park stood on the sites of Maynards and Bayside Bar and Grille including the adjacent parking lots.

Many locals remember the park. The Excelsior Amusement Park outlasted the Big Island Amusement Park by 42 years. The park had the usual fare of carnival rides like the Tilt-A-Whirl and roller coaster. It is probably most famous for Big Reggie's Danceland located across the street.

Even back then, Excelsior was a draw for big names. After opening in 1928, Danceland hosted major talent, including Tommy Dorsey, the Everly Brothers, the Beach Boys, and the Rolling Stones who were touring the United States for the first time.

Going into the 1960s, Big Reggie's Danceland started to experience tough times. It closed in 1968. The rest of the park followed in 1973. But, the Excelsior Amusement Park's run ended up in flames—literally. Arsonists destroyed the place a few months before its scheduled closing.

All that remains of the Excelsior Amusement Park is the concession stand which is now Tonka Trolley. Bayside Grille sits where the old picnic gardens were. But while you're here, stop in Bayside Bar and Grille. The restaurant has several photographs on display of the park. Be sure to park in its designated parking area.

Did You Know? While we have a different idea of what a casino is, the full definition from Merriam-Webster defines it as "…*a building or room used for social amusements*." Some later establishments may have had gambling—especially the blind pigs. But they typically offered more innocent activities like music or roller skating.

687 Excelsior Blvd, Excelsior

952-474-1113

baysidegrille.com

***

Snapshot of the 1910s

- 1910: Old St. Louis Hotel site became the 27-room mansion, Walden, built for Walter Douglas of Quaker Oats who later perished on the *Titantic*

- 1911: The Lake Park Hotel in Excelsior closed down

- 1911: President William Howard Taft toured the Lake Minnetonka area

- 1911: Big Island Amusement Park closed

- 1911: The first bridge spanning the Narrows channel was constructed

- 1912: The 142-foot steamboat, *Minneapolis*, was burned like the Excelsior in 1909, attracting a greater crowd that included visitors from the Twin Cities

- 1912: Mound is incorporated

- 1913: The Excelsior City Council authorized its first speed trap

- 1914: St. Albans Hotel burned down

- 1915: The Northland Inn in Wayzata was converted into an apartment house

- 1915: The Mound Depot was built

56

Experience Fine Craftsmanship at the Classic Boat Show

The Annual Bob Speltz Land-O-Lakes Antique & Classic Boat Rendezvous in September is a must-see event. See classic boats of all descriptions. You don't have to be a boat owner to appreciate the fine craftsmanship of these antique boats. Vote for your favorite. Held in September.

Tip: While Maynards has docks, the classic boats take up most of the space. I'd recommend not boating to the event but rather be a landlubber instead.

Maynards Dock
685 Excelsior Blvd., Excelsior
952-470-1800

Bob Speltz Land-O-Lakes Chapter of the Antique and Classic Boat Society
acbs-bslol.com

***

Boat Building on Lake Minnetonka

The Lake Minnetonka area has a rich history of boat-building. And it's easy to understand why. Of the famous names of the lake, one boat builder stands out, Sawin H. Dyer. Dyer began building boats in 1881.

Dyer came from Bangor, Maine. Before settling on Lake Minnetonka, Dyer had many adventures. He had traveled to Central America and had visited Pike's Peak. He launched his first rowboats on Stubbs Bay. His son, Arthur, also acquired a knack for boat building.

Sawin Dyer worked on several prominent boats of the time, including the *Mary*, which was rebuilt after its horrific boiler explosion in 1880. It was rechristened as the *Hiawatha* in 1881.

But Arthur Dyer is probably most well known for his construction of the *Onawa*, on display at the Excelsior-Lake Minnetonka Historical Society. Dyer built the 26-foot sloop for Hazen Burton and his son, Ward.

The *Onawa* broke speed records when it hit the racing circuit with its "*gliding-over-the-water*" design and canoe-like body. Burton and his sloop won handily over his competition during its 1893 launch. Dyer's business, the Dyer Boat Works, burned down in 1910, taking 43 boats down with it.

57

Be a Tourist at the Blue Line Cafe

The Blue Line Cafe once stood at the site of the Bayshore Manor condos. Its name comes from the blue line around the gunwale of the rowboats it rented. The cafe had a 400-seat dining room. The Blue Line Cafe was located on Center Street when it was first built in 1878.

Then, the Blue Line Cafe was moved to its location on Water Street in 1903. While it lasted, the restaurant drew many tourists and locals. Like many buildings around Lake Minnetonka, fire destroyed the cafe in 1958.

Take a moment to look out from the Excelsior Dock at the end of Water Street. Then, as now, this area is the hub of activity. The charter boats carry out the tradition almost as old as the town of Excelsior itself. Take a seat at one of the benches, and watch the boat traffic.

Did You Know? The little round building at the docks, the Port of Excelsior, was part of the original Blue Line Cafe. It stands where it did during the cafe's stint. It was also Pappa's Lakeview Hamburger Stand for a time.

***

Where Did It Go?

Places and businesses come and go. But many towns on Lake Minnetonka took the expression literally. Some buildings like the Trinity Episcopal Church in Excelsior moved for the streetcar tracks. Others like the Deephaven Depot were carted off when they became obsolete. Here is a partial list of the the buildings and places that have had more than one location.

- *Wayzata*: St. Anthony Street moved

- *Tonka Bay*: Tonka Bay Casino (1883-1920) moved to Excelsior to become the Excelsior Park Ballroom, then, Big Reggies's Danceland

- *Upper Lake House*: Moved to Birch Bluff and became the Edgewood Hotel

- *Trinity Episcopal Church*, Excelsior: Moved from Third Street to Second Street in 1907 for construction of streetcar tracks

- *Camp Memorial Chapel*, Minnetonka Beach: Moved from the Camp Estate to its present location on County Road 15

- *Excelsior Depot*: Moved from Water and Third Streets to its present location

- *Mound Depot*: Moved from Shoreline Road near Lost Lake to its present location in Surfside Park

- *Third Street's high ground:* Removed in 1956 for Excelsior's east parking lot
- *Mann's Inn/Edgewood Hotel:* Moved farther down the Edgewood to Howard's Point
- *The Beehive,* former boarding house in Excelsior: Moved to its Third Street location in 1883
- *Pleasant Grove House,* 139-151 Second Street, Excelsior: A portion of the original hotel was moved to 185 West Lake Street after it closed
- *Deephaven Depot*: Moved to Park Avenue and remodeled into a private residence

Did You Know? The University of Minnesota rejected a proposal that would have moved its campus the to the Lake Minnetonka area.

58

Take the Excelsior Walking Tour

See Excelsior in a whole new way. Grab the map and stay with the tour. You'll visit 21 points of interest downtown and on the quieter streets off the main drag.

Learn about the old Excelsior Amusement Park and stories of the town's founding fathers and important people, like Captain John Johnson and Mister Jimmy. Brochures are available near the Port of Excelsior and the Trolley Depot near the library.

Note: While the tour is open to the public, the stops are not. Please respect private properties on the tour.

***

Discover the Historic Places of Excelsior

Did you notice the numbered plaques on some houses and buildings you passed during the walking tour? The Excelsior Historic Preservation Commission designated several structures around town historic sites. The commission recognized their contribution to the Excelsior you know today.

If you're looking for more history and interesting facts, look for the numbered houses. And for a more detailed look at the history of each one, check out the book, *Walking the Trails of History*, available the Excelsior-Lake Minnetonka Historical Society.

Note: While the tour is open to the public, the stops are not. Please respect private properties on the tour.

#1, Excelsior School, 261 School Avenue
#2, Wyer-Pearce House, 201 Mill Street
#3, Trinity Episcopal Church Chapel, 300 Second Street
#4, Excelsior Commons, Port of Excelsior
#5, Frank Perkins House, 332 Second Street
#6, Captain Johnson's House, 200 Second Street
#7, McGrath/Arey House, 193 Second Street
#8, Catholic Mission House, 217 First Street
#9, Enoch Dyer House, 180 First Street
#10, Porter/Dillman House, 175 First Street
#11, The Little Brown Cottage, 170 Lake Street
#12, Kalorama Cottage, 262-264 Lake Street
#13, Palmer's Grove, 140 W. Lake Street
#14, Milnor House, 6 Third Street
#15, Michael House, 205 Third Street
#16, Excelsior Fruit Growers Building, 450 Third Street

#17, Smith/Sampson House, 152 Maple Street

#18, Clark/Aldritt House, 371 Water Street

#19, A.W. Latham House, 634 Third Avenue

#20, Bennett/Studer House, 201 Second Street

#21, Willis Willard House, 152 Third Street

#22, Bennett's Livery, 432-438 Second Street

#23, The Phillips Building, 420 Second Street

#24, IOOF Lodge, 250-252 Water Street

#25, Sickler/Newman/Seifert House, 712 Galpin Lake Road

#26, Gould Greenhouse Office, 374 George Street

#27, Gould Greenhouse and Gould House, 440 Water Street

#28, The Beehive, 321-323 Third Street

#29, Rev. Samuel T. Show House, 192 George Street

#30, White House overflow, 429 Second Street

#31, Oak Hill Cemetery, North side of State Highway 7

59

Pay Respects at the Oak Hill Cemetery

Sitting high on a hill overlooking the city and St. Albans Bay is the Oak Hill Cemetery. The cemetery shows the history of the hardships of settlement in the Lake Minnetonka area. With its first burial in 1855, monuments on its grounds commemorate the early residents.

Visitors will also find a Civil War Monument. Other tributes honor the memories of the founding community members and military who served the country. The cemetery also includes the Galpin Monument.

The monument stands as a tribute to Charles Galpin who established the First Independent Church of Excelsior in 1853. It is a fitting memorial to a man who contributed so much to Lake Minnetonka and her people. The Excelsior Heritage Preservation Committee recognized the Oak Hill Cemetery for its unique record of past and its people.

Note: Please respect the cemetery and its grounds for what it is.

North side of State Highway 7, Excelsior

***

Wyer-Pierce House

The Wyer-Pierce House is worth a stop. It offers a stunning example of the upper class summer cottage found on Lake Minnetonka. It is the largest and best preserved. While you may scoff at the term, cottage, it embodies the essence of these homes however opulent.

Upper-class residents of Minneapolis and St. Paul escaped to the nearby lakes to get away from the hustle and bustle of city life. And in this regard, Lake Minnetonka played the ideal hostess.

James I. Wyer II left Minneapolis to live here after the house was built in 1877 by C.F. Warner. Described as steamboat Gothic, Fred Pearce, Sr. later took over ownership of the house, lending his name to the historic building's name.

Pearce was a legend himself, owning the Excelsior Amusement Park. The house was later remodeled into a duplex before becoming the bed and breakfast, Christopher Inn. It is now privately owned.

Both the National Register of Historic Places and the Excelsior Heritage Preservation Commission have recognized the unique character of the Wyer-Pierce House. Even the nearby streetlights are historic. One look, and you'll understand why these associations considered the Wyer-Pearce House special.

Note: The Wyer-Pierce House is a private residence. Look from the road only.

201 Mill Street, Excelsior

60

Pay Tribute to a Legend at the Captain Johnson Monument

The story of Captain John R. Johnson is part of the the lore of the steamboat era. Blanche Nichols Wilson described Johnson as "*Minnetonka's Sea Dog*," in her book, *Minnetonka Story*.

Of all the steamboat owners on Lake Minnetonka, Johnson stands out on many fronts, starting literally at the bottom. He started his career on the *City of St. Louis* as part of her crew. Johnson would later not only become her captain, but would own her.

The steamboat industry started to suffer from declining tourism in the late 1800s, especially at the larger hotels. Johnson saw an opportunity. He bought the fleet of the Lake Minnetonka Navigation Company which included some notable steamers such as the *City of St. Louis* and the *Belle of Minnetonka*.

Unlike the cruel fate of the *Belle of Minnetonka*, the *City of St. Louis* saw new life as scow and as the barge, *Priscilla*. Opportunity knocked again when Johnson constructed three ferries for the short-lived Big Island Amusement Park.

His days in the steamer business came to a quiet close. Instead, he concentrated his efforts on his other business, the Lake Minnetonka Dredging Company. It was here that he would leave his mark on Lake Minnetonka history.

Johnson's contributions exist on land and water. On the lake, his company deepened Excelsior Bay in 1902. Other cities around the lake can thank Johnson for dredging the present-day Narrows Channel. On land, Johnson built the roadbed for County Road 15 on north shore of Lake Minnetonka.

When Captain Johnson passed away in 1931, his body laid in state in the Masonic Temple. Stores and businesses closed for the funeral services. Later, the city of Excelsior commemorated Johnson with this memorial.

The memorial is a time capsule of Captain Johnson's life. The anchor came from the *Belle of Minnetonka*. The propeller is from the *Saucy Kate,* while the pilot wheel was once on the tug, the *John Alden.* Even the flag staff is tied to Johnson as one he once presented to a boys' club. Be sure to visit #62 for a bit more of Captain Johnson's legacy.

Did You Know? Boating was definitely in the blood of the Johnson family. Grandson, Anson Mase, went on to run his own excursion boat, the *Tonka Belle,* in a nod to the *Belle of Minnetonka.* He launched the boat in 1954.

Captain Johnson Monument
Lake Street and Excelsior Boulevard, Excelsior

***

The Legacy of the Steamers

The lake's first steamer, the *Governor Ramsey*, set the stage for what would become the steamboat era starting in 1860. With 13 steamers carrying 35,000 passengers in 1881, the tourism industry was about to take off.

Just two years later in the summer of 1883 between June 1 and October 1, 13 steamers carried over 90,000 passengers on the waters of Lake Minnetonka. At the height of the steamboat era, 97 steamers ferried visitors to stops around the lake including the many hotels that once existed.

Many hotels commissioned boats to transport guests along with attractions such as the Big Island Amusement Park. Others ran excursions, touring the various sites on the lake. The boats of the time were not small affairs. The largest of the steamboats, the *Belle of Minnetonka*, was 300 foot long.

Here are some of the notable steamers from back in the day of steamboats.

Belle of Minnetonka, 300 foot long, 2,500 to 3,000 passengers
Launched the day after grand opening of the Hotel Lafayette in 1882

City of St. Louis, 160 feet long, 1,000 passengers
Launched on June 4, 1881, the *City of St. Louis* was the largest steamer on the lake for a brief time and the first one over 100 feet. It was the first to be lighted by electricity.

Excelsior, 125 foot long
Launched in 1901. Originally a stern wheeler called *George*. It met its infamous end in 1909 when it was torched as a tourist attraction.

Flying Dutchman, 35 foot long
Launched in the 1880s. It would later become the ill-fated *Minnie Cook*. You have to wonder about the decision to call this boat—or any boat—the *Flying Dutchman*. Won't the legend of it being a doomed ghost ship give you a clue? Just saying.

Governor Ramsey, 50 foot side-wheeler
Launched in 1860. Built for Rev. Charles Galpin. It was the first steamboat on Lake Minnetonka. It would ends its days on the water as the barge, *Mermaid*.

Hattie May, 100 foot stern wheeler, 350 passengers
Launched 1878, largest steamer on lake until the *City of St. Louis*. It was the first stern wheeler on the lake.

Kate, 45 foot long propeller boat
Launched in 1876. It later sunk after its boiler exploded. The boat was recovered and rebuilt as the *Saucy Kate*. In 1899, a fire took her off the water.

Mary, 78 foot propeller boat, 125 passengers
Launched in 1876. Like the *Kate*, its boiler exploded and the boat was rebuilt as the *Hiawatha*. It left Lake Minnetonka in 1887 for Green Bay.

Sue Gardiner, 35 foot propeller boat
Launched in 1868 by Charles Gardiner. It was the first propeller boat on the lake and the second steamboat on the lake.

61

Spend the Day at the Excelsior Commons

The first impression you get of the Excelsior Commons is how big it is for a city park. And indeed, it is the only park of its size that you'll find along the lake. But confusion about the actual size exists. My research uncovered the commons described as 17 acres, 13 acres, and 15.5 acres.

Whatever the acreage, it's still is a popular destination and a tourist attraction itself. You have to thank the foresight of the founding fathers who set aside the parcel at a time when settlers were making claims around the Lake Minnetonka shore.

Charles Galpin proposed the idea of a commons area, adding to his influence in the Lake Minnetonka area. The cost in 1855 was $1.25 per acre. In today's money, you'd have to fork out a mere $32 an acre. The commons was later confirmed as a legal entity in 1904.

From its beginnings as a public grounds, the Excelsior Commons has expanded to become so much more. And like many places around the lake, it's had its share of changes. If you were here in before 1922, for example, you might dare to climb its 16-foot high diving tower or slide down the 50-foot water slide.

The Excelsior Commons has had several additions over the years. In the 1930s, a Works Progress Administration (WPA) project gave the parks its amphitheater and stone seats. Then, in 1976, a band shell was added to the Excelsior Commons. Today the city hosts Excelsior Summer Concerts here, one Wednesday each month.

You find so much at the Excelsior Commons. You can lay out and take in some rays at the Excelsior Beach. During the summer, you can take in a baseball game. Hungry? Grab a treat at the concession stand. Or do what everyone likes to do: just find a bench to sit and watch the lake.

Tip: There is metered street parking along the commons. Free parking is available on Water Street and in the city lots on both the east and west sides of the main drag. Public dock space is limited. And make sure you have quarters to feed the meters.

Did You Know? The S.H. Dyer's Boat Works once stood on the site of the Excelsior Beach.

Concert information: City Hall, 952-474-5233

***

Lake Levels

If you think you've seen low water on Lake Minnetonka, then you probably weren't around in 1934. The lake levels dropped dangerously low. Kids waded across Excelsior Bay from Solberg's Point by St. Albans Bay to the site of the present-day city dock. The normal lake level is 929.4 feet above sea level. In 1934, it dipped below 922 feet.

Around 1990, the lake also experienced lower levels, but not quite as dramatically. The lake level fell under 926 feet. The lake has since recovered, with water levels hovering near the Normal Ordinary High Water level (OHWL).

According to the MN DNR, OHWL means:

"the ordinary high water level is an elevation delineating the highest water level that has been maintained for a sufficient period of time to leave evidence upon the landscape, commonly the point where the natural vegetation changes from predominantly aquatic to predominantly terrestrial;

for watercourses, the ordinary high water level is the elevation of the top of the bank of the channel; and

for reservoirs and flowages, the ordinary high water level is the operating elevation of the normal summer pool."

Information from the MN Department of Natural Resources
dnr.state.mn.us

62

Go See for Whom the the Bell Tolls

The bell of *Belle of Minnetonka* is one of the few bits that remains of the largest steamer ever on the lake. After all the pageantry and hype with its launch in 1882, its life on the lake only lasted 10 years. Its demise coincided with the declining tourism, especially at the grand hotels.

When the boat was dismantled in 1892, some remnants of the mighty steamboat made to the junk heap. Others were salvaged for other boats. And yet other parts ended up on the bottom of St. Albans Bay.

You can thank the citizens of Excelsior for having the foresight and love of the lake's history to buy back the bell in 1899. The bell then became the school bell at the Excelsior Public School. Later, it was moved to its present location behind the Excelsior City Hall.

It stands as a silent reminder to the steamboat era, the captain of the finest steamer on Lake Minnetonka, and the historic Excelsior Public School.

339 Third Street, Excelsior

***

Notable Lasts

Things come and go. When things disappeared around Lake Minnetonka, it often denoted the end of an era or way of life. The lake has seen many of these changes over the years. Here are a few of the notable lasts around the lake.

- *Sampson House*, 500 Second Street, Excelsior: When it closed in 1960, it was the last of Excelsior's original hotels

- *Gleason House*, corner of Lake Street and Walker Wayzata was the last of the lake hotels to go in 1964

- *Hotel Del Otero*, Spring Park, was the last of the grand hotels to go when it burned down in 1945

- *George V. Thomson house* in Deephaven replaced Donaldson house, the last of the large summer cottages built on the lake in 1926

- *Northland Inn*, Wayzata: Last of hotels from this era built on Lake Minnetonka

Walk on the Bottom of Excelsior Lake

The city of Excelsior didn't let hills get in the way of change; neither did it let a lake. Take a walk in downtown Excelsior on the west side of Lake Street.

Begin at the Port of Excelsior. Cross Lake Street and turn right onto the west side of the street. Then next block after Water Street, the main drag, is Center Street. Turn left, heading away from the lake. The next street on the right is 1st Street. Turn right. The next block on your left is Courtland Street. Turn left.

Follow Courtland Street. Notice something odd? You're walking downhill, but not just any hill. Keep following it as you pass Bell Street, then Third Street. You just walked the lake bottom of Excelsior Lake. To get back to town, turn left at 3rd Street. Water Street is three blocks away.

The lake was drained to make room for housing. The bowl-shaped depression is all that remains of the lake that once existed here. Other things on the 101 list also mention buildings that were moved and hills that were leveled. The Excelsior you see today is a far cry from what it once looked like.

Note: Please respect private properties.

***

The Bays and Lakes, Oh, My!

The history of Lake Minnetonka is written in the names of its bays and landmarks.

Black Lake
Cities: Spring Park and Mound
Based on an alleged American Indian tradition that said, "*The moon never shines on Black Lake.*"

Browns Bay
Cities: Orono and Wayzata
Named after James Brown, an early settler from Kentucky who built his cabin on its shore.

Carmans Bay
City: Orono
Named after John Carman, another one of the early settlers and the first resident of Orono Township. Carman would later become the first superintendent of School District 85 in Minnetrista. He was also the father-in-law of Mathias Cook, the owner of Cook's House in Mound.

Carsons Bay
City: Deephaven
Named after Elijah Carson, brother of American frontiersman, Christopher Houston "Kit" Carson of dime novels fame—allegedly

Coffee Cove
Cities: Spring Park and Orono
In the early days, you could only access Coffee Cove via West Arm.

Cooks Bay
City: Mound
Named after Mathias S. Cook whose log cabin eventually became the Lake View House and later Cook's House, one of Mound's most well known hotels

Crystal Bay
Cities: Orono and Minnetonka Beach
Named by Allen French, a Quaker from Ohio, who was awed by its beauty and water clarity. It is the deepest bay of the lake.

East Upper Lake
Cities: Orono, Shorewood, and Tonka Bay
The Narrows Channel connects the upper and lower lakes.

Echo Bay
Cities: Orono and Tonka Bay
Echo Bay is located between Lafayette Bay and Lower Lake South.

Emerald Lake

City: Mound

Like several connected lakes, Emerald Lake was not connected to Cooks Bay as it is today. Rather, you could access it only via Seton Lake. However, many boaters may not realize that the two are separate entities, i.e., unless they've noticed its sign on the bridge.

Excelsior Bay

Cities: Excelsior and Greenwood

Named after Henry Wadsworth Longfellow's poem by the same name

Forest Lake

City: Orono

Appropriately named for its heavily wooded shoreline. It became part of the lake proper when a channel was dredged to West Arm

Gideons Bay

Cities: Excelsior, Shorewood, and Tonka Bay

Named after horticulturist, Peter Gideon, of Wealthy apple fame

Grays Bay

Cities: Minnetonka and Wayzata

Named after Amos Gray, one of the earliest settlers on Lake Minnetonka. Gray built the first steam sawmill and store in Wayzata in 1854. He was the brother-in-law to both William and Joseph Chowen of Deephaven.

Halsted Bay

Cities: Mound and Minnetrista

Named after the Frank and George Halstead who were known as the hermits of the lake. The present name, Halsted, is a corruption of the family name, Halstead.

Harrison Bay
Cities: Mound and Spring Park
Named after boat builder, Captain Nathanial Harrison. Harrison designed and built steamers, including the *May Queen* and the *City of Minneapolis*. The former would later be destroyed when its boiler exploded in 1879

Jennings Bay
Cities: Minnetrista and Mound
Named after Frederick Jennings, a printer from New York

Lafayette Bay
Cities: Minnetonka Beach, Orono, and Tonka Bay
Named after the Lafayette Hotel, built by James J. Hill

Libbs Lake
City: Minnetonka
Located on the eastern side of Lake Minnetonka, this body of water was isolated from Lake Minnetonka's Grays Bay until a channel was dredged in the 1800s. As with Forest Lake, boat access is limited due to the canal and height of the Grays Bay Blvd bridge, which runs over the channel.

Lost Lake
City: Mound
Named for its slow wake channel that connects Cooks Bay to Mound. The channel was dredged after much discussion when the city center moved from the steamboat landing to the railroad station

Lower Lake North
Cities: Deephaven, Greenwood, and Orono
Has the dubious distinction of being the final resting place for three of Lake Minnetonka's historical streetcar steamboats: the *Como*, the *White Bear*, and the *Hopkins*

Lower Lake South
Cities: Deephaven, Greenwood, and Orono
Lower Lake South is located north of Excelsior Bay. Big Island is located in its waters

Maxwell Bay
City: Orono
Named by John Maxwell's family who built their cabin on this bay in 1854

North Arm
City: Orono
Its name comes from its geographical location on the lake that connects to Maxwell Bay to the east and Crystal Bay to the south

Old Channel Bay
City: Tonka Bay
Named for the original channel that connected upper and lower Lake Minnetonka

Peavy Lake
City: Wayzata
Named after Frank H. Peavey and once part of his Highcroft Estate. Though not originally a part of the lake, a channel was dredged that connects it to Browns Bay

Phelps Bay
Cities: Minnetrista, Mound, and Shorewood
Named after Carrington Phelps, a settler from Connecticut who owned land on what is now Phelps Island. The bay is unique in that it is surrounded by the four islands: Spray Island, Enchanted Island, Shady Island, and Wild Goose Island

Priest Bay
Cities: Minnetrista and Mound
Named after J.D. Priest, who had his farm on this bay

Robinsons Bay
Cities: Deephaven and Woodland
Named after Alfred B. Robinson whose farm was located here. Robinson and O.E. Garrison first laid out Wayzata

St. Albans Bay
Cities: Excelsior and Greenwood
Named by Enos Day, a native of St. Albans, Vermont, who came to Excelsior in 1856

St. Louis Bay
City: Deephaven
Named by Charles Gibson, a lawyer from St. Louis. It became the site of his famous Hotel St. Louis and his own magnificent, Northome. Despite its small size, there are two Lake Minnetonka Yacht Club's islands located here, Lighthouse Island and Bug Island

Seton Lake
City: Mound
Named for the Catholic saint, Elizabeth Ann Bayley Seton, known as Mother Seton. She was the first US citizen canonized by the Catholic Church. It was also a stop on the railroad.

Smiths Bay

Cities: Minnetonka Beach and Orono

Smith Bay is located between Lower Lake North and Crystal Ball. You'll find Bracketts Point in this bay.

Smithtown Bay

Cities: Victoria and Shorewood

Named after the the three Smith brothers, who were early settlers on Lake Minnetonka, originally staking claims in what is now Cooks Bay

South Upper Lake

Cities: Shorewood, Victoria, and Minnetrista

South Upper Lake is located north of Smithtown Bay.

Spring Park Bay

Cities: Mound, Orono, and Spring Park

Named after the city that shares its name

Stubbs Bay

City: Orono

Named after the Henry Stubbs Family, who farmed this area

Tanager Lake

City: Orono

Formerly known as Mud Lake, Tanager Lake is a quiet little lake, located west of Browns Bay.

Wayzata Bay

City: Wayzata

Named for the city that shares its name

West Arm
Cities: Mound, Spring Park, and Orono
Named after its geographical location, which is east of Harrison Bay
and west of Coffee Cove

West Upper Lake
City: Minnetrista

64

Take a Bite at Excelsior's Apple Day

There's no better way to celebrate the legacy of apples and the area's famous horticulturist than enjoying the day at Excelsior's Apple Day. And it's all about the apples. Enter your grandma's recipe in the apple judging contest. Or join the pie-eating contest if you'd rather be on the receiving end.

Held in September, the one-day event features a 5k and 1-mile Fun Run. And that's not all. Artisan vendors have lots to share at the street fair which runs the whole day. Each year brings new events and things to do. There's even the obligatory Beer and Wine Garden. It's a day to celebrate the contributions of early settlers like Peter Gideon and Charles Haralson.

Contact: Excelsior Chamber of Commerce, 952-474-6461
excelsior-lakeminnetonkachamber.com/apple-day.html

***

Excelsior Hotel History – Part 1

The history of hotels in Excelsior is unique because it had more places to stay than all other villages around the lake combined. Most places were smaller, accommodating far fewer guests than the grand hotels like the Hotel St. Louis or Hotel Lafayette. The majority were modest affairs. Like other villages, Excelsior had many boarding houses.

From a navigation standpoint, Excelsior was an easy jaunt from Wayzata, with no channels to navigate. And it was far enough away from the stench of the locomotives to feel like a vacation. It truly was—and is—a getaway.

The owners of the hotels had stories as exciting, salacious, and entertaining as the hotels they ran. Perhaps the most interesting stories concern the owner of the Fred Hawkins Hotel and Cafe. You can still see the name of the establishment on the side of the building at 235-237 Water Street toward the top.

Hawkins came to the area from Minneapolis. His place wasn't a resort with chartered boats or fishing excursions. Rather his hotel was a popular saloon and pool hall with rooms for guests staying the night upstairs.

To say that Hawkins had legal issues would be a gross understatement. It wasn't long before the Minneapolis saloon owner would get into the infamous Wets versus Drys battle. During his time in Excelsior, he got arrested seven times and get ensnared in 15 lawsuits.

The legality of liquor in Excelsior shifted back and forth with the vote. In 1897, the Wets won. The battle over the sale of intoxicating liquors was hardly new. In any village where the debate ensued, accusations of ballot stuffing were bandied around.

The victory of the Wets hardly lasted longer than a hangover. In 1905, the Drys outlawed the sale of intoxicating liquors, forcing Hawkins to close his saloon. But once a Wet, always a Wet.

Hawkins got pinched for selling liquor, giving the village the excuse it needed to shut Hawkins establishment for good. He later returned to Minneapolis where the battle of the Wets and Drys had been settled in favor of the Wets.

65

Ladies Night Out!

Thursday nights during the summer are something special in Excelsior. Enjoy specials and deals at the restaurants and businesses in downtown Excelsior that stay open later to cater to the ladies. But it's not just for the ladies. All are welcome to enjoy the energy and fun that makes Excelsior such a great place to visit.

Held every Thursday evenings, June through August
Contact: Excelsior Chamber of Commerce, 952-474-6461

***

Excelsior Hotel History – Part 2

The list of hotels reads like a laundry list of the movers and shakers of the area, with plenty of stories along the way. While not complete, the hotels and the history that follow provide a glimpse into the tourist trade as it waxed and waned in Excelsior.

Unlike the history of the Mound hotels, the stories about the Excelsior businesses are more complete, with a few exceptions. And the city and its townsfolk have done an outstanding job of recognizing its past and increasing awareness of the area's rich history.

Many hotels changed ownership several times in their run, typically with a name change. Hotels with multiple names are separated by "/" to reflect these changes.

The Hotels:

- *Appledore/Vermont House/American House/Central Hotel*, west side of Water Street near corner of Second Street, (1879-1895)

- *Beers Hotel/Spaulding House/Windsor*, Water and Second Streets, (1887-1897)

- *Blue Line Hotel/Stetson House/Hotel Degroodt/Belle Alto/ Donaldson House/Hotel Bay View*, 274 Lake Street, (1875-1913)

- *Degroodt's Summer House*, 238-240 Third Street, (1875?-1887)

- *Mann's Inn/Edgewood Hotel/Rustic Home*, Birch Bluff, (?-1906)

- *Excelsior's White House/Jenkins House/Frank Bardwell Hotel*, 1 Water Street, (1866-1921)
  Excelsior (1872-1946)

- *Fred Hawkins Hotel*, 235-237 Water Street, (1903-1913)

- *Galpin House/Excelsior House/La Paul Hotel/Goodrich House/ Excelsior Bay Hotel*: (1854-1928)

- *James H. Clark House/Well-Come Inn/Knowlton/Aldritt House*, 371 Water Street, (1858-Present as Bird House Inn)

- *Kalorama Cottage*, 262-264 Lake Street, (1882-?)

- *Long View House*, 200 block of Lake Street, (1881-1891)

- *Maple Inn*, 441 Second Street, (1901-1906)

- *May Place/Beacon Hill House/Mix Hill House*, corner of Minnetonka and Excelsior Blvds, (1877-1901?)

- *Pleasant Grove House*, 139-151 Second Street, (?-1886)

- *Prospect Hill,* (1868?-?)

- *Slater House/Sampson House*, 500 Second Street (1884-1961)

- *St. Albans Hotel and Health Resort*, Greenwood Circle, (1912-1914)

- *The Beehive/Sheldon Hall*, 321-323 Third Street, (1857-Present)

Bird House Inn
371 Water Street, Excelsior
952-474-0196
birdhouseinn.com

66

Party Like It's 1919 on the Trolley!

Excelsior embraces its past. The Excelsior Streetcar Line is a perfect example. The original service began in 1905. Trolleys ran from Lake Harriet through Hopkins to Excelsior through the town's main thorough way, Water Street.

Today, the Excelsior line includes two active cars and two in restoration: *Duluth* #78 (1893), *Twin City Rapid Transit streetcar* #1239 (1907), *Winona, MN* #10 (1913, being restored), and the *Mesaba Railway* #10 (restoration pending).

The line begins running in early May, weather permitting. There is a modest charge for the 15-minute tour. Please note that the streetcars do not run in the rain, nor are they handicap accessible. Reservations are not necessary.

The line also runs several special event trolleys, including its Story Time Trolley, Ghost Trolley, Trick r' Trolley, and Christkindlsmarkt event on Thanksgiving weekend. The trolleys are available for charters.

While you're there, be sure and visit the Excelsior-Lake Minnetonka Historical Society Museum.

Between 3rd and George Streets, Excelsior
General Information: 952-922-1096
trolleyride.org

***

The History of the Depot and Trolleys

The Minneapolis and St. Louis railway built the first Excelsior station in 1883. The Minneapolis, Lyndale and Minnetonka Railway had begun service to Excelsior in 1882 with up to six round trips daily until 1887. Then, the Great Northern Railway brought the motor line and ran trains. In 1902, it changed ownership once again and became part of the Twin City Rapid Transit Company (TCRT).

The TCRT started the streetcar line to Excelsior with cars entering on Lake Street and going through town on Water Street. The service ran until 1932 when the buses replaced it. Train service to Excelsior continued with the Minneapolis & St. Louis trains until it stopped servicing the area in 1960.

The present depot was built in 1952. It replaced the original depot located 20 feet to the west. The building has housed the Excelsior-Lake Minnetonka Historical Society since 1982.

Did You Know? In 1895, there were only seven listed phones on the lake.

67

Get Lucky at the Luck O' The Lake Race

It's never too early to start the racing season. The March Luck O' The Lake Race sees to that. But it is more than a 5k race. Don't be surprised if you see everyone getting in touch with their inner Irish heritage with the wearing of the green.

It is the first of the three races in the Lake Minnetonka Running Series. The others are the July 4th Firecracker Run and the September Park Nicollet Apple of the Lake 5K.

But to call the Luck O' The Lake Race just a race would do it an injustice. After the race, participants and the public are welcome to the tent party at Jake O'Connors. You'll be treated to live music and food available all day long. Even if you don't run the race, the tent party is a blast!

Did You Know? The inspiration for the name of Water Street came from a creek that ran from Galpin Lake to Lake Minnetonka. Who knew?

Starts and Ends on Water Street, Excelsior
excelsior-lakeminnetonkachamber.com/luck-o-the-lake.htm

***

The Wets and the Drys – Part 1

A tumultuous relationship existed between the so-called Wets and Drys in the Lake Minnetonka area. This is the same place where in 1902 you could get a sentence up to five days for spitting on the sidewalk in Excelsior. In 1873, Excelsior took its first vote on the issue, ending with a victory for the Drys.

But they weren't content with only liquor. In 1878, the Drys also set their sights on a ban of snuff, cigars, and all other tobacco. On the liquor front, they won again on another vote in 1896. But victory was short lived for the Drys. In 1897, the Wets emerged victorious. Alas, the licenses came with an 11 p.m. closing time.

Even with the victory for the Wets, tensions still persisted. Drys won the vote in 1905 in Excelsior. In 1906, even advertisements for intoxicating beverages were forbidden. Perhaps saloon owners took some comfort in the fact that milk sales also required a license in 1909. But just when you thought the matter was settled, tensions erupted once again. With another vote, the ball was in the Wets' court.

In 1912, D.W. Kennedy was granted a license to sell liquor from the appropriately named Beers Building at Water and Second Streets. It set him back a mere $1,500, which in today's dollars would be over a staggering $36,000—for one year. Considering that a liquor license today can cost anywhere from $25 to $15,000 gives you an idea about what the Drys thought about the matter. You can still see the Beers name today on the side of the building.

The battle of the Wets and Drys played out even with the most unlikely of opponents. The Drys claimed victory over the most powerful man at the time, James Hill. As the story goes, Hill ordered cases of wine to celebrate the grand opening of his *pièce de résistance*, the Lafayette Hotel, in 1882.

But even his power and influence could not sway local authorities to grant him a license. Then, it was legal to sell intoxicating beverages in bottles for personal consumption. But if you wanted a drink by the glass, well, that was forbidden by law.

Hill, being the maverick he was, served liquor at his bar in the Hotel Lafayette. His bartender was arrested repeatedly. Wet votes allegedly had connections to the grand hotels. Given Hill's disregard for the law, it hardly seemed to be a stretch.

Hill's open defiance of the law soon caught the attention of journalist, Alfred Stewart Dimond. His criticism of its food and the blatant debauchery of its staff put Hill and his hotel in the sights of the Temperance movement.

Social pressure mounted against Hill. This negative publicity certainly wouldn't help the tourism industry. Finally, on Fourth of July 1886, Hill relented and stopped serving.

68

Art + Music + the Lake = Excelsior Art on the Lake Festival

The Excelsior Art on the Lake is an annual event in June, drawing artists and art enthusiasts from all around. And it's easy to see why. In addition to the captivating artworks in a variety of mediums, you can enjoy music and food from regional vendors during the two-day event. It's a lake tradition that celebrated its 36th year in 2016.

Excelsior Chamber of Commerce
952-474-6461
excelsior-lakeminnetonkachamber.com/art-on-the-lake.html

***

Snapshot of the 1920s

- 1924: Cottagewood Club House burned down

- 1924: The Mound City Hotel closed

- 1924: Hotel Keewaydin in Excelsior burned down

- 1925: US Bureau of Public Roads established Rte. 12 from Wayzata to Minneapolis

- 1925: Excelsior Amusement Park opens

- 1926: Three streetcar boats are scuttled after declines in ridership

- 1926: While vacationing with his mistress, Olga Hinzenberg, Frank Lloyd Wright arrested for on charges of violating the Mann Act of 1910

- 1926: Fire engulfs the entire lower end of Lake Street in Wayzata

- 1926: The Lamb Bros. Dry Goods Store in Wayzata is sold and becomes the Hart's Cafe at the site where Cov now sits

- 1928: The Galpin Hotel, Excelsior's first hotel, was destroyed by fire

- 1929: Wayzata adopted a home rule charter, becoming a city

69

Do the Brew Tour

Excelsior Brewing Company has evolved into more than just a neighborhood brewery. From its no-frills tap room to its live music to its iconic logo, the company has blossomed into a fixture in Excelsior. What more can you say about a company that combines two of the best things about the lake and makes it their October festival, Docktober Fest?

But your trip to Excelsior wouldn't be complete without a tour to see where the magic happens. Head on over to the brewery on Saturdays from 12 p.m. to 2 p.m. to tour the facility, no reservations needed. And these people take brewing beer seriously. All bartenders and ambassadors are Certified Beer Servers through the Cicerone Certification program. But before you starting asking "*Where can I get a job like that,*" take the tour and sample the suds.

421 3rd Street, Excelsior
952-474-SUDS (7837)
excelsiorbrew.com

***

The Wets and the Drys—Part 2

The battle of the Wets and Drys remained contentious all across the lake, being played out in each of the villages. In Wayzata, the Maurer House, later the Minnetonka House, had its own blind pig. A blind pig or blind tiger was essentially a lower class speakeasy. As the name might suggest, a blind pig operated like a front for an attraction like, well, a blind pig.

You'd pay your admission and then partake of a complimentary beverage. After all, you paid to see the pig not the booze. And then, there was Wayzata's E.B. (Bonnie) Gleason with his own blind pig and special concoction called, "*Hoptonic.*"

Alas, Gleason also ran afoul of the law for the second time in 1885. But perhaps he had the last laugh when he was appointed Village Marshall in 1891. What is a blind tiger, you ask? It's a speakeasy where the owner is unknown.

The whole matter of Wets versus Drys came to a head in 1915. Days before the upcoming election, the *Wayzata Register* advised its readership to vote against a liquor license for the village. The Drys won. On March 9, 1915, all the major villages around Lake Minnetonka went dry.

Prohibition formally began in the United States in January 1920 with the passage of the 18th Amendment. It lasted until its repeal by the 21st Amendment in December 1933. No irony there. But all things good and bad must come to an end. With the repeal of the amendment, Wayzata issued its first liquor licenses in 1933.

Did You Know? In 1899, Excelsior established a curfew for adolescents under 16 prohibiting them to be out without an adult after 9 p.m. from spring to fall. Two offenses carried a penalty of up to 10 days in jail. It was the same penalty one could get for going over the 5 mph speed limit on city streets. Ouch!

70

Let's Go Antiquing!

Like many small towns, Excelsior has its share of unique shops. Leipold's Gifts and Antiques and Country Look-In Antiques offer a wide selection of nostalgic antiques and rare finds. Each store has its own special flavor.

Leipold's selection includes collectibles and one-of-a-kind Lake Minnetonka souvenirs. At Country Look-In, you'll find lake-related antiques like old fishing reels and water skis. You're sure to spot that must-have piece!

Leipold's Gifts and Antiques
239 Water St, Excelsior
952-474-5880

Country Look-In Antiques
240 Water St, Excelsior
952-474-0050

***

Snapshot of the 1930s

- 1930: Wayzata Blvd becomes the most heavily traveled road in the state, averaging 8,140 vehicles daily

- 1930: Excelsior's Red Owl Store opened

- 1932: Bus service to Excelsior replaces streetcars

- 1933: With the repeal of the 18th Amendment, Wayzata issues its first liquor licenses

- 1934: Arey Memorial for Dr. Hugh Chester Arey, popular local physician, was dedicated

- 1935: Excelsior hosts its first annual Apple Day

- 1936: The horses of the village of Excelsior got saddled up for the last time, with the Council's decision to sell the team

71

Let's Get Crazy!

Check out the crazy good deals at the Crazy Days. Held in July, the four-day event promises the summer's best bargains. On Saturday, let the kiddies have their fun too at the Kids Day event. Enjoy summer treats while you browse the flea market held on Saturday.

Contact: Excelsior Chamber of Commerce, 952-474-6461
excelsior-lakeminnetonkachamber.com/crazy-days.html

***

Playing the Numbers Game

- Number of bays: 24

- Miles of shoreline: ca 125 miles

- Acres: 14034 acres, according to the MN DNR

- Maximum depth: 113 feet (Crystal Bay)

- Volume: 130,340,560,000 gallons

- Greatest width: 5.8 miles

- Greatest length: 10.9 miles between Halsted Bay to Grays Bay
- Number of anglers in 2015 fishing tournaments: 630
- Number of large-mouthed bass taken in 2015 fishing tournaments: 1,947
- Number of launches at public access points in 2010: 62,112
- Number of bridges over channels: 18
- Average number of boat launches per day during the summer: 420
- Zebra mussels invade the lake: Confirmed July 28, 2010
- Purple loosestrife invaded the lake: 1940
- Eurasian water milifoil invaded the lake: 1987
- 2014 total Eurasian water milifoil harvest in truckloads: 162
- Place among the 10,000+ lakes in Minnesota: 9th largest*
- Watershed area: 95 square miles
- Year in which all of Minnetonka shoreline claimed: 1855**
- Watershed area of Minnehaha Creek: 181 square miles in 27 cities and 2 townships
- Size of Minnehaha Creek subwatershed: 30,290 acres
- Length of the Minnehaha Creek from Lake Minnetonka to Minnehaha Falls: 22 miles
- Number of days before Minnesotans found out that Minnesota became a state after the Act of Congress: 2
- Number of steamboats on Lake Minnetonka in its heyday: 97
- Overall attendance at the Old Log Theatre: about 6 million theater goers

- Number of miles completed on the railroad in Wayzata when it was first built: 1

- Days you could spend in jail for spitting on any public sidewalk or building in Excelsior in 1902: 5

- Daily trains to Mound after 1887: 30

- Number of rooms at Hotel Lafayette: 800

- Names that Big Island has been known by: 6 (Wetutanka Island, Meeker Island, Cottage Island, Morse Island, Big Island or Morse's Island, and just Big Island)

- Number of birds housed in the aviary of the Big Island Amusement Park: 2,000

- Number of farms within Minnetonka Township in 1930: 403

*Some print sources and signage denote Lake Minnetonka as the 10th largest lake in the state. The MN DNR lists the lake as the ninth largest. I opted to go with DNR figures.

**Some sources put 1859 as this date instead

72

You Can't Always Get What You Want

Every town has a story, and Excelsior is no exception. The legend goes when the Rolling Stones came to Excelsior for a concert in 1964, Mick Jagger came to what was then Bacon Drug. Mister Jimmy was there too, hoping to get a cherry coke. But he was told they didn't have it. James Hutmaker, aka Mister Jimmy, supposedly told Jagger that "*You can't always get what you want.*"

Locals who knew Mister Jimmy say the story is true. The lyrics suggest it too. There's the drug store, the cherry coke, the prescription bit, and of course, Mister Jimmy. Other dispute it, saying the latter is a reference to the band's producer, Jimmy Miller. I'll leave it for you to decide. Believe it, or not.

By the Way: Speaking of rock-n-roll rumors, how about that other one? That scene in *Purple Rain* where Prince dares Apollonia to purify herself in the waters of Lake Minnetonka? Not! According to Kirk Hokanson, the location scout for the movie, "*That was actually the Minnesota River, just south of the city.*"

http://lat.ms/1Wu6S6L

Old Bacon Drug (site of Victor's)
205 Water Street, Excelsior

***

The Concert the Rolling Stones Probably Want to Forget

The Rolling Stones played at the Big Reggie's Danceland Ballroom at the Excelsior Amusement Park. To put the concert in context, the British Invasion hadn't taken off yet. The first American tour for the Beatles started in February 1964, just four months after John F. Kennedy's assassination. The Rolling Stones would first make it across the pond in June 1964.

Their start began rocky with the band even opening for a dog act at one time. Remember, the pop music of the time featured surf music and girl groups. The Beatles had already recorded their first hit, *Please, Please Me*. And during their tour, the Beatles were on the Ed Sullivan Show three weeks in a row. Even the news shows got into the act, reporting about Beatlemania sweeping the country.

The Rolling Stones didn't have a number one hit yet even in the UK. It would come later in the summer with their cover of *It's All Over Now*. And it didn't help coming to Excelsior on the heels of a successful Beach Boys concert. They appeared at the ballroom with none of the publicity that the Beatles had received.

At Big Reggie's, the bad boy band played to a "crowd" of 300, give or take. Contrast that with the Beatles who arrived at JFK Airport with over 3,000 cheering fans waiting.

The reception, while not hostile, was weak with some booing the group calling them Beatle wannabees. One concert goer later said that she hated the music and walked out, to which Mick Jagger would have said, "*You can't always get what you want.*"

73

Get Schooled at the Historic Excelsior Public School

The Excelsior Public School sits upon one of the few hills untouched in the town's early days. Built between 1899-1901, the site is symbolic of the importance that Excelsior placed on education for its children. It was a mission shared by other communities around Lake Minnetonka. In its beginning, it served both elementary and high school students, with 30 students in its first year.

The bell of *Belle of Minnetonka* hung in its belfry until it was determined a safety hazard in the aging tower. It was removed in 1962. The bell was then placed in its present location behind the Excelsior City Hall, #62. The nearly 15,000-square foot school continued its educational functions until 1964. Then it was subdivided into offices to house the administration offices for Minnetonka School District 276.

261 School Avenue, Excelsior

***

Excelsior
By Henry Wadsworth Longfellow

The shades of night were falling fast,
As through an Alpine village passed
A youth, who bore, 'mid snow and ice,
A banner with the strange device,
Excelsior!

His brow was sad; his eye beneath,
Flashed like a falchion from its sheath,
And like a silver clarion rung
The accents of that unknown tongue,
Excelsior!

In happy homes he saw the light
Of household fires gleam warm and bright;
Above, the spectral glaciers shone,
And from his lips escaped a groan,
Excelsior!

"Try not the Pass!" the old man said;
"Dark lowers the tempest overhead,
The roaring torrent is deep and wide!"
And loud that clarion voice replied,
Excelsior!

"Oh stay," the maiden said, "and rest
Thy weary head upon this breast! "
A tear stood in his bright blue eye,
But still he answered, with a sigh,
Excelsior!

"Beware the pine-tree's withered branch!
Beware the awful avalanche!"
This was the peasant's last Good-night,
A voice replied, far up the height,
Excelsior!

At break of day, as heavenward
The pious monks of Saint Bernard
Uttered the oft-repeated prayer,
A voice cried through the startled air,
Excelsior!

A traveller, by the faithful hound,
Half-buried in the snow was found,
Still grasping in his hand of ice
That banner with the strange device,
Excelsior!

There in the twilight cold and gray,
Lifeless, but beautiful, he lay,
And from the sky, serene and far,
A voice fell like a falling star,
Excelsior!

74

Sip a Fine Whiskey

Jake O'Connors Public House offers a great selection of some of the best Irish whiskeys and scotches for your sipping pleasure. The pub offers an authentic Irish public house experience with its wood furnishings and vintage ads. It oozes class in a friendly, homey kind of way. You'll feel as if you're in Ireland. And the food is pretty darn good too.

Note: Jake's patio is dog friendly

Tip: Public dock space available down the street at the Excelsior Dock with paid meters. Bring quarters.

200 Water Street, Excelsior
952-908-9650
jakeoconnors.com

Here's to the health of your blood.
Here's to the blood that gives you good health.
If your blood isn't healthy,
Your health isn't bloody,
So here's to your bloody good health.
Sláinte!

***

Prohibition on Lake Minnetonka

With all this talk of wets and drys, you know there are some prohibition stories on Lake Minnetonka. And you'd be right. While St. Paul was the bootlegging center of Minnesota, Lake Minnetonka also had a few cards to play. The lake had something of a reputation, with its litany of blind pigs. And of course, there was James J. Hill in open defiance of liquor laws.

Lake Minnetonka residents didn't need to look too far for the players behind the passage of Prohibition. In addition to the local temperance movement, there was Congressman Andrew Volstead from Granite Falls who sponsored the Volstead Act in October 1919. But those in want of a wee dram wouldn't let something like a Congressional amendment get in the way of a good time.

Several speakeasies existed on the lake on just about any bay you'd like. In Excelsior today? Fat Emma's on St. Albans Bay will set you up. Boating on Priests Bay? Be sure and stop at Martin Smaby's place. On the quiet side in West Arm? Don't forget to pop over to Fagerness Point for a tipple. And if you're anywhere near Minnetonka Manor, look up Blind Julia's.

Fast forward to today, and the story has done a 180. Not only is Excelsior selling liquor, but the Excelsior Brewing Company has Sunday sales of growlers of beer.

PART X

Greenwood

Greenwood is one of three communities found on the shores of St. Albans Bay. The others include Deephaven and Woodland. It was one of several villages that incorporated after World War II. Though small, these communities wanted to remain independent of Excelsior.

St. Albans had tried to do the same back in 1855, but failed. The pages of Former Names and Wiped Off the Map give you an idea of how many villages got absorbed into the surrounding towns.

Incorporated as a city in 1956, Greenwood is home to one of the most beloved places on the lake, the Old Log Theatre. Greenwood may be small, but its influence is felt across the lake.

75

Dinner and the Theatre

Enjoy some fine entertainment at the Old Log Theatre in Greenwood, the oldest professional theater in Minnesota. Opened in 1940, the theatre hosts a variety of productions. It mainly sticks to the screwball comedy flavor.

You can make a night of it with a pre-theatre dinner at the Cast & Cru restaurant which also serves non-theatre goers. Student and group pricing are available for shows. Performances run Thursday through Saturday evenings and afternoon matinees on Wednesdays and Sundays.

Maybe you have the theatre in your blood? You can become a volunteer usher and earn complementary tickets. Or if you really want to take the plunge, consider auditioning for an upcoming production. Check http://www.minnesotaplaylist.com for listings.

Old Log Theatre, LLC.
5185 Meadville St., Greenwood, MN 55331
952-474-5951
oldlog.com

Box Office Information
952-474-5951
Cast & Cru Reservations: 952-767-9700

***

Famous Lake Minnetonka Residents

Every place has its famous residents. And there's no shortage of them in the Lake Minnetonka area. Aside from entrepreneurs like James Hill, here are a few of our famous sons and daughters.

Mound:
Andrew Sisters

Minnetonka Beach:
Hal Van Every, NFL Football player, Green Bay Packers

Shorewood:
John Curry, Former Minnesota Wild Ice hockey goaltender

Deephaven:
Russell T. Wing, inventor of the Parker 51 pen, "*the world's most wanted pen.*" While not born on Lake Minnetonka, Wing moved to Cottagewood in 1938 before the 1941 release of the pen. Wing had a tornado-proof house built in 1966, one year after the devastating F4 tornadoes hit the Lake Minnetonka area.

Wayzata:
James Laurinaitis, NFL Football player, New Orleans Saints
Kent DuChaine, Blues singer

Did You Know? The Lake Minnetonka area has about a 30 percent greater risk of tornadoes than the rest of the state of Minnesota.

PART XI

Deephaven

Each town or village on Lake Minnetonka has its own character. Deephaven stands out as a vestige of the wooded shores of Lake Minnetonka of old. It has a distinctive park-like feel about it, reminiscent of the era of cottagers who built their summer homes to flee the pollution and noise of the city.

The abundance of small neighborhood parks in Deephaven adds to its charm. The village is 2.5 miles long, 1.5 miles at greatest width, and has about eight miles of shoreline. Contrast this with the Tonka Bay Hotel which had nearly five miles of shoreline.

Alice Burton, wife of Hazen Burton of Minnetonka Yacht Club fame, named the village. The name comes from a book of the same name by Sarah Orne Jewett. It tells the story of two women who spend a summer at a sleepy coastal village in Maine. Mrs. Burton had met Jewett earlier. Though not a Minnetonka story *per se*, its theme certainly fit the era.

Hazen Burton is synonymous with Deephaven and the the racing scow. He is perhaps most well-known for the first racing scow, the *Onawa*. Burton spearheaded the drive to get a train stop here. It made Deephaven the social destination it became. It also fueled the fight for railroad competition. The scenic beauty of this part of the lake drew many tourists, with its showcase hotel, the Hotel St. Louis.

After the hotel closed in 1907, Walter Donald Douglas of Quaker Oaks Company fame,and his wife, Mahala Dutton–Douglas, built their 27-room estate on the site. Alas, the tranquility of their home on the lake was shattered when tragedy befell the family on April 15, 1912.

Walter Douglas died along with 1,516 others with the sinking the the *Titantic*. His wife and her maid survived the disaster. She continued on at the estate, which they called Walden, until her death in 1945.

Today, Deephaven carries on this tradition as a peaceful and relaxing setting. It is a friendly village, which embodies the meaning of community.

76

Visit the Cottagewood Store

Built by Ralph and Stella Chapman in 1895, the Cottagewood Store is a fixture in Deephaven and important to the area's history. The village of Cottagewood was the first railway station on Carsons Bay. The store sold groceries and other necessities to travelers and hotel guests. When you first see it, you'll feel like you stepped into the past.

Many neighborhood grocery stores existed around the lake, not unlike the Cottagewood Store. The store survived through multiple ownership changes. But changing times threatened its existence. The Cottagewood Store seemed doomed to join this lot of other failed businesses.

Rather than see it destroyed, the residents of Deephaven rallied around its cause. They bought the building in 1995 after raising private funds. You can thank the wisdom of these generous people so that we all can enjoy this icon of the past. Today, the Cottagewood Store is more than a store; it is part of the community.

It hosts a slate of events open to the public including its Grill Nights on Friday summer evenings, its fall lawn sale, and Fall Fest event. It's worth a stop on any tour of Lake Minnetonka. Like its early days, the Cottagewood Store offers treats and snacks as well as build-your-own sandwiches.

20280 Cottagewood Avenue, Deephaven
952-470-8400
cottagewoodusa.com
Seasonal Hours

***

Chowen's Corner

Every town has its hub. Back in the 1870s, Chowen's Corner at the intersection of the present-day Highway 101 and Minnetonka Blvd was it for Deephaven. Chowen itself existed as a post office until 1891. It took its name from the Chowen family who members lived around the area. Proper pronunciation is *cow-ens*, not *chow-ens*.

Joseph Chowen from Pennsylvania was the original landowner of the area that bears his name. Like many settling in around Lake Minnetonka, he claimed his 160 acres. His brother-in-law, James Shaver, claimed the land to the north. George Chowen, his brother, had the land to the south of Joseph's. And William Chowen, another brother, had the land to the east of Joseph. It's easy to see why the name Chowen's Corner was a natural segue.

Chowen's Corner evolved from a place where the family lived to a business section in 1906. It began with the Deephaven Store which later became the Deephaven Market in 1926. More businesses sprang up in the area, including Mason's Motors, Schroeder's Dairy, the Log Cabin Cafe, and a barber shop.

By 1940, 12 businesses occupied the corner. But this age of prosperity was not to last. The Deephaven Market became the Deephaven Grocery Store from1927 to the 1940s. Dosch's Oil Station lasted for a short sprint between 1970 and 1975. Several changed ownership over the years. Some moved to other locations, leaving few reminders of Deephaven's own *"Busy Corners."*

Did You Know? Thorpe Park was once the Bennis truck garden.

77

A House with a View

A favorite local pastime is to view the houses from the water. Many of the great homes are located on private roads, making them hard to see by land. However, you'll still be in for a treat looking at them by boat.

Robinsons Bay is a good place to start your tour of some of the grandest houses. From Robinsons Bay, boat north toward Wayzata Bay. Other prominent features include Breezy and Cedar Points.

Robinsons Bay was named after Alfred B. Robinson, an early settler of the area who farmed here. Like many Lake Minnetonka residents, Robinson served during the Civil War. In June 1862, he was discharged for a disability.

But he still felt the draw to serve his country. He re-enlisted and became a musician until he was mustered out three years later. His other claim to fame was his part in first laying out the village of Wayzata with O.E. Garrison.

248

This small bay takes you off the beaten track from Wayzata Bay to the rest of the lake. You'll find Robinsons Bay Beach here, one of several small neighborhood beaches on the lake. Another landmark is Gibsons Point, named for Sir Charles Gibson of Hotel St. Louis fame. You can read more about Gibson's story and contributions to the lake on the page for the Hotel St. Louis on #79. Smaller bays like Robinsons Bay are worth a stop.

Note: Please respect the privacy of residents living along the shore

Did You Know? Deephaven was home to the first Frank Lloyd Wright house in Minnesota. Commissioned by Francis Little, a banker from Chicago, the house was intended to be a "summer retreat cottage." It represented a fine example of Wright's concept of "*organic architecture.*"

Subsequent owners wanted to tear down the house because of its quirks, typically of Wright houses. Fortunately, the efforts of private individuals spared the house. The Metropolitan Museum of Art houses the former living room. A hallway resides at the Minneapolis Institute of Arts. The home was only one of a dozen Wright designed and built in the state.

Location: Robinsons Bay

***

Snapshot of the 1940s

- 1940: The Tonka Theater opened
- 1940: The Old Log Theatre opened
- 1941: Red Owl Grocery Store on Water and Second Streets burned down, but reopened four months later
- 1944: Wayzata outlaws outdoor privies
- 1945: Hotel Del Otero burned down
- 1945: The Tonka Theater burned down, later to be rebuilt
- 1946: Mound Metalcraft (predecessor to Tonka Toys) is created in Mound, MN
- 1949: Wayzata celebrates is Days of '49 festival with a hole-in-one tournament, torch-light water show, canoe derby, and the highlight, the crowning of guests, Bob Hope and Cedric Adams, as honorary ranch hands

78

Relax at Carsons Bay

If you're boating, Carsons Bay is off the beaten path away from the hustle and bustle of the lake. This A-grade bay offers a marvelous setting for snorkeling. Farther into the bay, quiet waters make for a peaceful place to anchor, and enjoy some rays.

The bay also has its own story. Word around the lake is that the bay was named after none other than, Elijah Carson, brother to the American frontiersman, Christopher Houston "Kit" Carson of dime novels fame. However, the local folklore may be off the mark. Elijah lived in Maine for his first 30 years, while Kit was born in Kentucky. Oh, well, it makes for a good story anyway.

Elijah settled in the Deephaven area in the early 1850s and owned over 100 acres here. Residents around the bay are probably pretty happy Carson came along to lend his name to the bay. Before being called Carsons Bay, it had been known as Pig Inlet.

Location: Carsons Bay, southeast side of the lake

***

Public Boat Launches

There are numerous neighborhood launches around the lake. But parking is iffy or sometimes non-existent at some locations. The best place to launch is at a public dock. It's free, and parking typically is available. Be prepared for long waits on weekends and holidays. MN DNR personnel will conduct an inspection of boats for invasive plants and zebra mussels.

Spring Park Bay
Grays Bay Dam
North Arm Bay
Carsons Bay
Phelps Bay
Cooks Bay
Grays Bay
Halsted Bay

Did You Know? Weekends and holidays account for over 50 percent of all boat launches, with an average of 504 a day.

79

Experience the Hotel St. Louis at the Deephaven Beach

Deephaven Beach offers the closest thing you'll get to visiting the Hotel St. Louis. Though long gone, you can still experience what a visitor from back in the day would have seen. The hotel was located on the large hill behind the beach.

Imagine the steamboat, *City of St. Louis*, dropping off guests to stay at the grand hotel. As you walk along the shore, you're enjoying the views and fresh breezes off the water just like anyone visiting back then.

Deephaven is a beautiful place, with residents who appreciate the treasure they have. Parking at the beach and most of the parks is by permit only May through October. Non-residents can park at nearby Thorpe Park and walk down to the beach. It'll give you a chance to experience the tranquility of this village and its scores of large trees that preserve its park-like feel.

St. Louis Bay, Deephaven

***

The Hotel St. Louis (1879–1907)

Why St. Louis, you ask? Well, there's a good reason for that. Sir Charles Gibson of St. Louis purchased the land in this bay. He built his Hotel St. Louis here. As the story goes, Emperor Franz Joseph of Austria gave him the title of the Knight in Austria in 1882. Likewise, the German emperor awarded him the Commander's Cross the of the Royal Prussian Crown.

These honors recognized his legal efforts of 30 years earlier in a case involving the power of the government and establishing its autocracy. Others referred to him as the *"Father of the Lake"* for his many contributions. Suffice to say, he was well known and well respected both locally and abroad.

For Gibson, the hotel provided a quality place to stay for visitors to the lake. As an account from the August 7, 1878 *St. Louis Times* had noted, the lake offered, *"…beggarly accommodations and indigestible meals…"* Something had to be done. Gibson was no stranger to the hotel business, having previously owned one in St. Louis.

Gibson did two things that would change the lake and the village of Deephaven. First, he built his palatial *Northome* summer home which was completed in 1877. After all, what's a summer home without friends to enjoy it with? And Gibson had a friend list that any Facebook user would envy. So, he then built his masterpiece.

The first of the grand hotels of Lake Minnetonka, the Hotel St. Louis opened in 1879. For its time, it was state-of-the-art, boasting electric lights, a bath on every floor, and later, telephone service. The hotel had the *"plumbing of the highest quality."*

Like many of the hotels of the day, it attracted southern guests, anxious for relief from the blistering summer heat. Guests could either take a train directly to the hotel. Or they could stop at the Deephaven Depot and take a carriage. Gibson's goal was to create this scenic haven, while making it convenient for travel.

To put its size in perspective, the Radisson Blu Hotel in Minneapolis has 360 rooms compared to the Hotel St. Louis's 200 rooms. But the Hotel St. Louis would win over the Radisson if it existed today. The three-story hotel offered stunning views of the lake. As an entrepreneur and hotel keeper, Gibson knew his stuff. He had rescued a hotel in St. Louis earlier, ironically enough after a fire.

Gibson continued his involvement in affairs of the lake. During the 1880s, he became embroiled in the contentious issues surrounding navigation, dams, and water levels. Gibsons Point in Robinsons Bay recognizes his achievements and love for the lake.

As you look out over the bay, you probably can see what made it so delightful. The calmer waters on St. Louis and Carsons Bays offered a quiet respite from city life. It helped having the view of the yacht club as well. But its luxurious life was short-lived. Gibson realized that the end was near and tried to sell the property to Hennepin County. He hoped the county would make it a park.

The high price tag nixed the sale. So, instead, Gibson formed a syndicate to subdivide and sell the land as lots. Unlike the fires that would take the Hotel Lafayette and Hotel Del Otero, the wrecking ball took those honors for the Hotel St. Louis.

The site later became the Walden Estate for Walter Douglas of Quaker Oats fame. As for Northome, it became Cedarhurst, built by R.M. Bennett at the site. The land since has come to the same fate as the hotel, having been subdivided.

Charles Gibson had continued to support the Lake Minnetonka area throughout his life. And fortunately, he didn't witness the razing of his grand hotel. He died on October 27, 1899, ironically enough, at a Minneapolis hotel.

Tennis, Anyone?

Looking for something more active? How about a game of tennis at Deephaven's Haralson Park? The 0.5-acre park features one of the few public platform tennis courts in Minnesota. The courts have heat below the decking, intended to keep the courts clear. They are not meant to heat the area.

Constructed in 2008, it offers a great place to start your exploration of this quiet little village on the lake. And when you get done with your game, take a leisurely stroll down the LRT trail to take in more of the town.

As you may have guessed, the park is named after Charles Haralson of apple fame and the former superintendent of the University of Minnesota Fruit Breeding Farm. He moved to Deephaven in 1922.

Note: Dogs are not permitted at Haralson Park

Did You Know? If you drive, bike, or walk the neighborhoods of Deephaven, you'll like come across the Northome arch built in the 1900s. This massive stone arch is hard to miss. But when you look at it, you'll see something is amiss. Its left arch was removed in 1925 to allow trucks to pass through. Then, in 1987, the road improved, and the remaining part of the arch was restored.

Next to Deephaven Village Hall across from the LRT Trail
20225 Cottagewood Road, Deephaven

***

Deephaven's Hotel History

Deephaven wasn't a major player in the hotel business, at least terms of the number of hotels. However, its few hotels stand out as icons. Samuel C. Gale built the Maplewood Inn in 1869, located south of Breezy Point. It was the first hotel built on the lake for summer only use. The hotel offered affordable and informal accommodations. The Maplewood Inn was a popular place until it burned down in 1901.

Another popular hotel on the lake was the Cottagewood Club House. Built in 1885, it had the second phone in Deephaven with the Hotel St. Louis having the other. For a mere $8 to $12 a week, you could enjoy a comfortable Lake Minnetonka vacation.

The hotel was sold after 1900 and became the Keewaydin Hotel. Its name comes from Longfellow's poem, *Song of Hiawatha*, meaning northwest wind. The Keewaydin Hotel burned down in 1924, the last of the Deephaven hotels.

Of course, the grandest of them all was the Hotel St. Louis located on the shores of the bay of the same name. Opened in 1879, it was the first of the grand hotels on the lake. Before its demise, furnishings within the hotel were sold off. In 1907, it was demolished. One can only hope that a bit of the Hotel St. Louis lives on in some lake homes.

Cottagewood/Keewaydin Hotel (1885-1924)
Maplewood Inn (1869-1901)
St. Louis Hotel (1879-1907)

PART XII

Woodland

Woodland's story is similar to Greenwood. Settled in 1882, the village is just over a half square mile in size. While Greenwood resisted annexation by Excelsior, Woodland did the same with Wayzata.

The community was a stop on the streetcar line called Maplewood. The station has since been converted to a private home after the line stopped running in 1932. Despite its small size, it is not the small kid on the block. Woodland is among the top 50 towns with the highest income in the United States. It is one of the wealthiest cities in Minnesota.

Incorporated in 1948, the city is a residential community that celebrates its heritage as part of the old Maplewoods summer residence and the Groveland Homeowners Association.

PART XIII

General Things

Some things you can't pin down to a particular bay or town. So, there is this list of general things to do. Some of them exist all over the lake area like geocaching. Other are found in a few places like pontoon rentals or cruises. And yet, others are seasonal in nature like the Fourth of July or Tour de Tonka.

But the great thing about them is that you have more opportunities to see and do different things around Lake Minnetonka. You can keep coming back again and again. No two visits to the lake are the same. Each visit is worth a story.

81

Let's Go Geocaching!

It's a secret known by geocachers around the world. If you want to find the cool, off-the-beaten-path type of places, then go geocaching! Geocachers love a good story. And they all want their hides to stand out as unique and fun.

All you need is a GPS unit or a GPS-enabled phone for this high tech game of hide-and-seek. Then download the c:geo app for your smartphone. Sign up for a free account at geocaching.com, and you're ready to go!

You can search for a cache by any of the names of any towns on the lake. Setting additional parameters in the Advanced Search can filter cache size, difficulty, type, and radius of search. A five-mile radius will get you plenty. Caches are located at posted coordinates, but it's not as easy as it sounds. And that's the fun.

The central coordinates for the lake are at the Big Ambitions on Big Island (N 44° 55.946/W 093° 33.519). As you might guess, some caches like those on the island require a boat. But there are many others that will lead landlubbers around the lake.

Location: Just about everywhere around the lake

***

Stations and Stops On the Way to Lake Minnetonka

What was it like to travel by train to Lake Minnetonka? If it were 1902, this is one of routes you would have taken via the Great Northern trains. Sounds a lot faster than commuting from St. Paul today!

Leave St. Paul: 1:35 p.m.
Leave Minneapolis: 2:00 p.m.
Leave Wayzata: 2:20 p.m.
Leave Ferndale: 2:24 p.m.
Leave Orono: 2:28 p.m.
Leave Markville: 2:31 p.m.
Leave Arcola: 2:34 p.m.
Arrive Minnetonka Beach: 2:36 p.m.
Arrive Langdon Park: Stop on signal
Arrive Spring Park: 2:40 p.m.
Arrive Mound: 2: 45 p.m.

82

Let's Go Fishing!

Fishing Lake Minnetonka became great sport early on in the Golden Age of Tourism. Create your own fishing party to relive these days of sport. Lake Minnetonka is known for good bass, walleye, and muskie fishing. I can personally attest to the former. But if pan fish are more your style, there's plenty of sunnies, perch, and crappies.

The great thing about fishing Lake Minnetonka is that each lake is different. They vary in size and depth. You'll also find different levels of clarity, vegetation, and of course, water quality. Back in the day, few people had cottages on the lake. The city folk would come out to Lake Minnetonka and enjoy a one-day fishing excursion. Follow in their footsteps. Let's go fishing!

When you get your fishing license, learn the rules of the lake. Lake Minnetonka has some rules unique to it. And you'll certainly want to know your limits. In 1909, this fact alluded John O'Connor who was arrested for having five lines in the water. He ended up doing 10 days in Carver County Jail for his indiscretion. And no jail cell has a lake view. Enjoy the day! Enjoy the sun! And try for that record bass!

Prefer someone to show you the ropes? Hire a fishing guide to lead you to the best spots. And you don't have to limit yourself to the summer. Ever thought about going ice fishing? Here's your chance!

Did You Know? The Minnesota Department of Natural Resources issues between 450 and 600 permits annually to fishing tournament organizers.

Erickson Guide Service
Contact Person: Kurt Erickson
5025 Avon Drive, Mound
612-801-5058
info@ericksonguide.com
ericksonguide.com

***

Fishing Piers Around the Lake

There are several small city park fishing venues. To get you started, here is a list of Minnesota DNR sites. Remember the rules; you need a fishing license on Lake Minnetonka.

Mound
Pier. In Mound, take Cty Rd 15 to Belmont Ln., go N 1 block, turn right on to Lynwood Blvd. Go to Centerview Ln, turn right and go 2 blocks to pier in city park

Coffee Channel
Platform. In Spring Park at the intersection of Co Rd 19 (Shadywood Rd) and Co Rd 51 (Sunset Dr); shore fishing available

North Arm Public Access
Platform. In Orono at the intersection of Co Rd 51 & 19 at the Hennepin Co public boat access; shore fishing available

Tonka Narrows Channel
Platform. In the city of Tonka Bay, on Co Rd 19 about 1 mi S of Co Rd 15 (Shoreline Dr) at the bridge over the Narrows; shore fishing available

Lake Minnetonka Regional Park
Pier. In Minnetrista, from Hwy 7 & Co Rd 44 go N on 44 about 1/2 mi to the Hennepin Co park entrance on E side of road; pier is next to boat access

Maxwell Bay Public Access
Pier. In Orono at Maxwell Bay public access at Co 51 and Tonkawa Rd (County 135)

St. Albans Bay Bridge
Platform. In Excelsior on Minnetonka Blvd, N of Excelsior Blvd.; shore fishing available

Public fishing access is also available at the Wayzata Public Beach.

Pier information from the MN DNR website

Did You Know? Carp from Germany were *stocked* in Lake Minnetonka in 1880, in hopes that it would add to the plethora of game fish. And we all know how that ended up.

83

Cruising Lake Minnetonka Style

Taking a cruise on the lake is, dare I say, a luxurious way to enjoy the lake in style. And you'll find a variety of options, themed cruises, and plenty more. Each cruise line offers different experiences, with some offering dining options.

Most offer both public and private cruises. Remember, cruises are popular, so reservations are strongly suggested. And a word to the wise: it can be chilly out on the water, especially during evening cruises. Take a wrap and be prepared.

Al and Alma
5201 Piper Road, Mound
Office: 952-472-3098
al-almas.com

Bayview Event Center
687 Excelsior Blvd, Excelsior
952-470-VIEW (8439)
http://bayviewevent.com

Lady of the Lake Paddlewheel Boat Cruises
Docked in Excelsior

952- 929-1209

612-803-5580

ladyofthelakecruise.com

Paradise Charter Cruises
2 Water St, Excelsior

952-474-8058

Toll Free: 888-559-8058

twincitiescruises.com

Seanote Cruises
Excelsior Dock

8 Water Street, Excelsior

952-944-7464

seanotecruises.com

Steamboat Minnehaha
Museum of Lake Minnetonka

37 Water Street, Excelsior

952-474-2115 (messages only)

Wayzata Bay Charters Inc.
687 Excelsior Blvd., Excelsior

952-451-9001

wayzatabaycharters.com

***

Boating Stats

Seeing all the boats on the lake may make you wonder how busy does the lake get. Ask a Minnetonka boater. And they'll tell you, "*Busy. Very busy.*" Actually, most boaters on the lake think that the boat traffic is just about right.

As you might guess, weekends and holidays are peak boating times. They account for over half of the public access launches, with 2.5 times more boats hitting the water than during the week. So, if you're looking for a quiet time on the lake, weekdays offer a better option.

The Minnesota DNR and the Minnehaha Creek Watershed District keep tabs on the lake's goings-on. A 2010 report by the DNR tallied over 62,000 launches at public access sites to give you an idea about numbers. But what about actual boats on the lake?

Though dated, a report by the two agencies surveying boating trends from 1984 to 2004 gives some insight. Other than fluctuations due to weather, the stable numbers contained in this report provide a good baseline. Boating on Lake Minnetonka is a different experience than other lakes.

For one, boating densities are greater, reaching four or five times that of other popular lakes such as the Brainerd Lakes. Second, boaters, well, boat. We're not anchoring in one place as often for fishing or the like. We're on the go. The report puts this figure at 2:1, moving versus still.

So, how many boats are on the lake at a given time? The average falls anywhere between 907 and 1,453 boats on a summer weekend afternoon. But the numbers fall like an anchor dropped from your boat going into the early evening hours. The average counts are about one-third of peak afternoon numbers. Weekday boating differs, with numbers dropping after 6 p.m. and later.

The next thing you might ask is where are they? The east and northwest portions of the lake tend to have the greatest concentrations of boats. They may have upward of 60 to 80 percent more boats than the southwest areas of the lake. These figures are also reflected in the number of launches at public access docks.

The takeaway message is this: if you want lots of activity and opportunities to socialize with other boaters, head east or northwest from the launch. If you want a quiet day on the water, seek out those southwest bays, especially on a weekday.

Minnesota DNR and the Minnehaha Creek Watershed District
Report
http://files.dnr.state.mn.us/aboutdnr/reports/boating/
minnetonka_boatingtrends.pdf

84

Run a Race!

If you're into running—or fun runs—the Lake Minnetonka area has plenty of opportunities to get your race fix. Here are a few of the many opportunities to show your stuff

Excelsior
Luck of the O' Lake (March)
5K Color Run (May)
Lake Minnetonka Triathlon (June)
Firecracker Run (July)
Apple of the Lake (September)

Wayzata
Lake Minnetonka Marathon (May)

Mound
Running of the Bays 5K Run & Half Marathon (September)

Lake Minnetonka Running Series
Luck of the O' Lake (March)
Firecracker Run (July 4th)
September Park Nicollet Apple of the Lake 5K (September)

***

Keep an Eye on the Weather

When you live on the lake, you become more weather conscious, especially if you are a boater. It pays to know how to read the skies. Whether you're boating or shopping, take a cue from the Boy Scouts. Be prepared.

Wind

- North wind: Cold weather on the way

- South wind: it's going to warm up

- East wind: Oh, boy. Weather is on the way

- West wind: It's clearing up

Cloud Cover

- Cirrus: wispy clouds + wind from any direction but west = rain in 24 hours

- Stratus: low gray clouds mean the weather is going to take a turn for the worse

- Cumulus: big puffy white clouds mean pleasant weather, unless the wind is coming from the east

Folklore

- If chickweed flowers are open, it'll be clear for hours
- My grandma swore by this one. If your cat washes behind its ears, it's going to rain/snow

85

Tour the Historic Burwell House

Tour the Burwell House, and learn about Lake Minnetonka's early beginnings and its burgeoning mill industry. For a special experience, attend the Burwell Festival, held on the fourth Saturday in June. The event includes entertainment and free tours of the house.

Looking for a Christmas event? Visit the Holiday Open House on the first or second weekend of December to see the house with its Victorian finery.

13209 E. McGinty Road, Minnetonka
minnetonkahistory.wix.com/minnetonkahistory

***

The History of Minnetonka Mills

The history of settlement of the Lake Minnetonka area begins in Minnetonka Mills. Simon Steven built the first claim shanty in 1852. Minnetonka Mills is interesting for what it isn't. Other than the Burwell House grounds, little exists of the thriving mill operation that once was here.

First, Minnehaha Creek is only a shadow of the larger navigable waterway that it once was. Who would believe that the Minnehaha Creek once supported boat traffic?

Second, there wasn't a dam. Setters completed the dam at Minnetonka Mills in 1853. Grays Bay wouldn't have a dam until 1897. The Grays Bay dam caused the disappearance of the mill pond and steamboat traffic. You can see the aftermath at the Burwell House, where the front yard used to slope down to the shoreline.

Minnetonka Mills had a shaky start. In 1858, its sawmill and furniture factory burned down, dooming its future. But Minnetonka Mills recovered from fires with the railroad in 1867. Then, regular steamboat runs began between Excelsior and Minnetonka Mills in 1874. Despite its rapid rise, Minnetonka Mills soon faded into memory.

86

Canoe the Minnehaha Creek

For an up close view of Minnehaha Creek, canoe the length of the Minnehaha Creek beginning at its starting point at Grays Bay. Your five to six-hour trek will take you through wetlands and towns, past mill sites and parks. It winds up with a spectacular finish at Minnehaha Falls.

But you don't have to canoe the entire creek. Find a short stretch to get your canoeing fix to match your experience level. The creek can be a challenging adventure, especially after heavy rains and during high water.

The Minnehaha Creek Watershed District (MCWD) provides a detailed map with points of interest, portages, and parking sites along its path to help you plan your trip. Parking is limited. They also have a hotline for current creek conditions. For a real Lake Minnetonka adventure, relive the experience of early explorers, Joseph Brown and John Snelling.

Launch at Grays Bay Dam
Current conditions: 952-471-0590
minnehahacreek.org

***

From the Song of Hiawatha

By Henry Wadsworth Longfellow

With him dwelt his dark-eyed daughter,
Wayward as the Minnehaha,
With her moods of shade and sunshine,
Eyes that smiled and frowned alternate,
Feet as rapid as the river,
Tresses flowing like the water,
And as musical a laughter:
And he named her from the river,
From the water-fall he named her,
Minnehaha, Laughing Water.

87

Ride the Tour de Tonka

From its humble beginnings in 2006, the Tour de Tonka has evolved into a high-class regional event. The 2015 tour attracted over 3,500 participants. Unlike the 2,276 mile-Tour de France (2014 figure), the Tour de Tonka has your choice of seven distances: 15, 28, 40, 48, 57, 67, or 100 miles. And it's a ride, not a race.

The Tour de Tonka is a whirl-wind tour of 23 different west metro communities, including most of the towns surrounding the lake. The ride goes on rain or shine. Twelve rest stops along the way will give you time to catch breath and have a snack. There is a fee to enter the ride. Participants are also encouraged to donate to the ICA Food Shelf Donation. The ride takes place in August. Sign up. Enjoy the ride. See the sights.

Note: Dogs are not allowed at the event, with the exception of service dogs

General Questions and Registration: 952-401-6800

***

The History of Biking Minnetonka

Along with the tourism industry and the hotels, bicycling had a similar rise in popularity in the early 1880s in the Twin Cities. It wasn't long before bicyclist, or wheelmen as they were called, made their way to the scenic views of Lake Minnetonka. Both men and women took to the sport, forming bicycling clubs.

The first bicycle race was held in 1896. Participants began at the Hotel St. Louis on St. Louis Bay in Deephaven and eventually made their way to Park Avenue, in Minneapolis. But bicycling become more than recreation.

The bicycling sector itself became a strong political coalition. As their numbers grew, so did the cries for more biking paths. And, then, as now, the competition for the roadways followed. First there were the farmers and then, the horseless carriage. It's a battle that persists today with the scores of *"Share the Road"* signs.

Do a Studio Tour

Lake Minnetonka is home to a vibrant and talented art community. During the Lake Minnetonka Studio Tour, artists open up their studios to allow visitors to view art first hand and speak with the talent behind the work. You can experience art in a variety of mediums, including painting, ceramics, and sculpture among a host of other works. Held in spring, the two-day event is a must-see for art lovers!

LakeMtka-StudioTour.com

***

Snapshot of the 1950s

- 1952: Present Excelsior Deport building built
- 1954: Deephaven got its first dial phones

Fourth of July on the Lake

Lake Minnetonka offers one of the best ways to celebrate the Fourth of July that you'll find anywhere. As locals will tell you, some of the best fireworks on the lake happen in the bays far from the town celebrations. If you want to avoid the crowds on the water, try finding a quiet bay and drop anchor. And just wait for the fireworks to begin.

But if you'd rather celebrate on land, Lake Minnetonka has plenty of options. While smaller ones exists, I've included some of the larger venues. Be aware that parking fills up fast—as does the seating at restaurants. It's a good time to enjoy some street fare or pack a picnic lunch.

Wayzata
Fourth of July Flying Pancake Breakfast, kiddie parade, mini olympics
Yes, it means what it says. Vets eat free
Wayzata Depot and Railroad Museum
402 Lake Street E, Wayzata
wayzata.org

Excelsior
Excelsior Commons
Events include: kids parade, petting zoo, sand sculpture contest, Firecracker 5k run
100 percent community funded
excelsior-lakeminnetonkachamber.com/lake-minnetonka-4th-of-july.html

***

"It has always been my private conviction that any man who pits his intelligence against a fish and loses has it coming."
– John Steinbeck

90

Drop Anchor!

Sometimes, the best things to do on Lake Minnetonka don't require any effort at all. Find a quiet spot on a bay. Drop anchor and just relax.

Have fun boat-watching while sipping a cold beverage. Let the waves lull you to sleep for the best nap you'll ever have. Pack a lunch and make it a day! Need to cool off? Jump in the lake! Everyone's doing it. Stay close to the boat and never go in the water without a flotation of some kind, whether it's a PFD, a raft, or even a noodle.

Tip: When planning your boat outing, the east side of the lake tends to be busiest and the southwest, the quietest.

Bonus Tip: If you're new to boating, remember the sun reflecting off the water makes for some intense rays. Don't forget to pack the suntan lotion and apply often.

Location: Any quiet bay

***

Where to Swim?

August has warmest water temperature for Lake Minnetonka. It can reach upward of 80 degrees Fahrenheit. What are the warmest bays? Stubbs Bay, followed by Maxwell and Carsons Bays top the list, according to the 2014 Minnehaha Watershed Conservation District's Lake Minnetonka Subwatershed Report.

As for the chilliest, if you really want to cool off, make sure and head over to Spring Park Bay, followed by Wayzata and Cooks Bays for a refreshing swim.

But of course, any bay will do when you feel the itch to get in the water. If you're looking for a good place to hang out and spend the day, you might want to consider one of these popular locations.

Maxwell Bay
Wawatosa Island
Big Island
Wild Goose Chase Island

Or our personal favorite, Carsons Bay

Personal Tip: Personally, I won't take to the water until the temperature is at least 70 degrees. Any lower and it's a difficult first step off the ladder.

91

Pontoon It!

If you've never boated Lake Minnetonka, you are in for a treat. It doesn't get any better than taking to the big water. And a pontoon boat is a great way to get your feet wet.

Rentals, especially on weekends and holidays, book quickly. Make a reservation as soon as you decide a date. And check on rainy day policies. You don't want to be the one boat on the water when storms are in the forecast.

Note: Several of these marinas rent other watercraft, such as jet skis. Marinas vary with their age requirements, restrictions, grilling, and pet policies. Most prohibit tubing, skiing, wake boarding, or knee boarding. But that's no problem. You're here to see the lake, right?

Bay to Bay Boat Club
135 Lakeview Ave, Excelsior
952-401-3880
baytobayboatclub.com

Howard's Point Marina, Inc.
5400 Howard's Point Road, Shorewood
952-474-4464
howardspoint.com

Metro Lakes Marina
4850 Edgewater Drive, Mound
952-472-9595
metrolakesmarina.com

Minnetonka Boat Club and Rental
952- 472-1220
minnetonkaboats.net

Rockvam Boat Yard
4068 Sunset Drive, Spring Park
952-471-9515
rockvamboatrentals.com

***

Being a Good Boater

Boater's etiquette

- Don't buzz anchored boats

- Maintain at least 150-foot distance from other boats, especially when people are in the water. You'll appreciate the returned courtesy next time you're anchored, drinking a cool beverage

- When a boat passes you, maintain your current speed. This isn't the time to crank it up

- Respect sailboats and slow-moving watercraft

- When anchoring, give other boaters space; it's not a parking lot
- Boaters help other boaters; give them a hand if you see someone having engine problems on the water
- Not everyone enjoys your taste in music; keep it down or move someplace else
- Don't forget that sound travels very well and very far on the water. Just saying.
- Don't tube, water ski or jet ski in a bay or cove already filled with anchored boats; there's a whole lot of lake out there to enjoy
- Don't harass the wildlife or waterfowl; they're just trying to make a living too.
- Pack out all of your trash; don't spoil the lake
- If towed by someone on the water, offer cash. If towing, decline it. It's what we do as boaters
- If you meet a guy named Dave driving an old dilapidated boat, tell him we said hi.

Don't Get Boarded by the Sheriff's Water Patrol

- Learn what a gunwale is; stay off of it when the boat is underway. That also applies to the bow, transom, or decking over the bow, unless there is railing
- No wake means no wake
- Follow the speed limits; yes, there are speed limits on the water (Day: 40 mph, Night: 20 mph, 5 mph slow minimum wake in marked quiet waters areas, within 150 feet of shore, within 150 feet of swim areas or swimmers, scuba flags, or docks (except dock from which operating)

- Check your lights often; better yet, keep spare bulbs on board

- Make sure the little ones have life vests on; yes, even if they don't like it

- Don't give the water patrol a reason to board your boat; don't act stupid

- While you can drink on the boat, your pilot is still subject to DWI laws while underway

- Personal watercraft like jet skis, are subject to all of the same laws as boats. In addition, you can only legally operate one from 9:30 a.m. to one hour before sunset. Operators under 18 must have a watercraft operator's permit or an adult on board.

- Be polite if boarded; they're just doing their job. Besides, don't you think they'd rather be boating too rather than tooling around watching everyone else have fun?

I'm not suggesting that the water patrol surveys boats with binoculars, but if you want your boat trip to not include a Breathalyzer, a call to your lawyer, or bail, then keep these tips in mind. Better yet, look over the DNR Boating Guide before you go out.

Boating Guide
http://files.dnr.state.mn.us/rlp/regulations/boatwater/
boatingguide.pdf

FYI: Peaking boating hours are between 2:00 p.m.and 7:00 p.m. during summer weekends and from 5:00 p.m. to 10:00 p.m. during the week.

Note: There is a curfew on Lake Minnetonka. Unless Mom or Dad are with you, anyone less than 15 years old cannot be on the lake from 10 p.m. to 6 a.m. Teens 16 to 17 years old cannot be on the lake from 12 a.m. to 6 a.m. Sorry, the law is the law.

92

Go Island Hopping!

While most islands are private, a few are open to the public. Here's your chance to do some island hopping. The Three Rivers Park District owns and manages three islands on the lake: Wild Goose Chase Island, Wawatasso Island, and part of Big Island.

All are undeveloped, though you will find trails on most. Feel free to fish or picnic on the islands. Rules specific to each island are posted.

Restrictions that apply to all islands include: no overnight camping and hours from 5 a.m. to 10 p.m. And don't think you can let that 10 p.m. closing time slide. The Hennepin County Sheriff's Water Patrol keeps a watch on the islands.

Note: Parts of Big Island include the Big Island Veterans Camp and private residences. Please respect all restricted areas

Wild Goose Chase Island, Spring Park Bay
Wawatasso Island, South Upper Lake
Big Island, Lower Lake South

***

The Islands – Part 2

Gale Island (Lower Lake South)
See Gale Island, #49

Lighthouse Island (St. Louis Bay)
This island was created when the bay was dredged and the channel opened for the site of the Minnetonka Yacht Club clubhouse

Mahpiyata Island (Lower Lake South)
Created by one-time owner, Olaf Searle, by digging a channel through Big Island

Phelps Island (Phelps Bay)
The largest island on Lake Minnetonka.

Shady Island (Phelps Bay)
The 150-room Hotel Harrow opened in 1880 on the island. It became the home of the Shady Island Association. Formerly named Rockwell Island, the remains of the steamboat, *May Queen*, once owned by Captain Rockwell, remain the rear of the island

Spirit Island (Wayzata Bay)
Said by the Dakota to guard the north shore of the entrance into Wayzata Bay

Spray Island (Phelps Bay)
Privately owned. Despite its small size, a little pond exists on the island.

Wawatosa Island (West Upper Lake)

Like Crane Island, Wawatasso Island had its own share of nesting birds. But a 1944 storm took out the nesting trees. As far as its distinctive name, it may be a corruption of yet another name from the *Song of Hiawatha*, Wah-wah-taysee, the little fire-fly.

Wild Goose Island (Phelps Bay)

Once owned by James Hill's railroad

Smaller Islands

Bell's Island (Wayzata)

Duck Island (Gideons Bay)

Frog Island (Gideons Bay)

Pelican Island (Spring Park Bay)

93

Get a Map

Even if you're an old salt, having a map of Lake Minnetonka makes sense. There's so many places to see! Follow along the stories in this book with a map to guide the way. If you're new to the lake, a map is essential for finding the sites. Every landmark, bay, and point you find on the map has a story.

But some of the stories are still being written, like your story. Our map is covered with our own notes of special places. I'll leave it to you to discover where our personal landmarks. A few of our favorites are Puppy Cove/NSFW, Belly Bruise Bay, and Buzz Bayou. You can find maps at any of the marinas on the lake.

Location: The whole lake!

***

Remembering the Past

Many of the names and places of the present hearken back to Lake Minnetonka's early days. Here are just a few of the ones you may encounter on or off the water.

Arlington Heights, Wayzata: Site of the Arlington House

Black Lake: Based on an alleged American Indian tradition that said, *"The moon never shines on Black Lake."*

Bracketts Point: Formerly known as Starvation Point in reference to oral history of a trapper starving there. It was later purchased by George Brackett who originally named it Orono. The point served as the site for early sailing regattas.

Edgewood Road: Reference to the Edgewood Hotel on Birch Bluff, one of the latest hotels that closed in 1947

Ferndale: Coined by James Hill in reference to the abundant ferns growing there. Many of the founding fathers of the milling industry built homes in this area

Gluek's Point: It was named for the Gluek brothers who brewed near-beer during Prohibition. Tragically, John Gluek and his wife, Minnie, were killed in 1908 at a train crossing after leaving their home. It was the first accident involving an automobile and train on the lake.

Hardscrabble: Named in honor of an early settler to the Lake Minnetonka area

Harrington Road, Wayzata: Appropriately named for John Stevens Harrington who laid out Wayzata's first road. John Harrington Stevens would later be known as the *"Father of Minneapolis."* Harrington Road was originally Ferndale Road. A cross street took on the name Harrington Road. Confused yet?

Maplewood: Reference to the abundance of maples in the area

Navarre: Named from a park in Paris, which was named by a knight of Navarre who later became the King of France

Northome: Literally, north home of Sir Charles Gibson of St. Louis

Palmer: Named after the Palmer House, a hotel that opened in 1887 by John and Nellie Palmer. It was known as a sportsmen resort and a *"sanitarium for hay fever patients."*

Saga Hill: A reference to the cooperative formed in 1885 by Norwegian Americans looking for a summer retreat on the shores of West Arm

Seton: Stop on the railroad; Named for the Catholic saint, Elizabeth Ann Bayley Seton, known as Mother Seton. She was the first US citizen canonized by the Catholic Church. Like her namesake, the area included Seton Guild, a summer residence for girls

Three Points: An area dominated by summer cottages. The three points refer to Dreamwood, Woodland, and Shadywood. The streets are named after birds.

Zimmermans Pass: Named for Commodore Zimmerman who purchased land in the area in 1877. He ran the Lake Minnetonka Navigation Company, which owned several steamers in a partnership with James Hill.

94

Playing It Safe

The Minnetonka Power Squadron, a unit of the United States Power Squadrons, offers both public and members-only boater safety courses that will teach you what you need to be safe on the water. You can take a public class or a self-study boating course. You might even consider a membership to join other like-minded boaters.

Lake Minnetonka boaters agree. A Minnesota DNR survey of boaters found that 49 percent think that all boaters should be required to take a boater safety class. I did. And you don't need to boat for long before you may find yourself thinking the same. The BoatUS Foundation also offers a free online course.

Minnetonka Power Squadron
612-568-BOAT (2628)
minnetonkaps.org

BoatUS Foundation
boatus.org/courses/

MN DNR

dnr.state.mn.us/safety/boatwater/education.html

***

Boating Tips

The goal of any boating trip is to have a great, safe time. Here are a few of my favorite boating tips.

- Take a tip from NASA; check the weather before you launch

- Activate weather alerts on your phone

- Head back to dock as soon as you get a weather alert. It takes a lot longer to get back than you think—especially when everyone else is doing the same thing

- Don't touch anything metal on your boat during a thunderstorm. But why are you still on the water, anyway?

- Pack a lunch for the boat, especially on busy weekends or holidays. A table is one thing; a place to dock is another thing all together

- Have spare light bulbs on the boat for *all* your lights

- Make sure you have quarters and dollar bills, your choice of denomination for tips or the docking meters at Excelsior Dock. Wayzata Public Docks are free

- Keep a boat log to remember your adventures on the water

- Keep current to-go menus of all lake restaurants on your boat. Nothing beats dinner on the water!

- Get a tow buddy. He's your boater friend who you can call for a tow on the water anytime, day or night—and vice versa!

- When anchoring, make sure your anchor is secure

- Avoid going through Coffee Cove around dinner time. Everyone else has the same idea

- Plan wisely. Westward travel on the lake near sunset is brutal. A hat or visor is essential gear

- *Always* remove your fenders after you launch your boat. Only noobs leave them on.

- Talk like a boater. You dock a boat, not park it. They are lines, not ropes. And yes, they are fenders, not bumpers

95

Fall Overboard!

For the best snorkeling on the lake, let the Minnehaha Creek Watershed District (MCWD) guide you. The MCWD monitors water quality of the creek's watershed which includes Lake Minnetonka. The grade gives you an idea of how clear the water is. It also provides a guide about the water quality and how it may affect your time on the water. The surveys grades many aspects of the water with a summary letter grade.

The bays you want to snorkel in are those with an A grade. According to the MCWD, this designation means: "*Crystal clear, beautiful. These lakes are exceptional and can be enjoyed by recreation users without question or hesitation.*" You can also opt for B-graded bays which are generally good. However, algae may present a problem later in the season.

The A-graded bays according to MCWD's 2015 report are:

- St. Albans Bay
- Grays Bay

- Lower Lake South

- Lower Lake North

- Maxwell Bay

- North Arm

- Phelps Bay

- Smithtown Bay

- Wayzata Bay

- Gideons Bay

- Carsons Bay

- Wayzata Bay

- Lafayette Bay

- Spring Park Bay

- West Upper Lake

- Crystal Bay

- Cooks Bay

The B-graded bays according to MCWD are:

- Black Lake

- Priests Bay

While you can certainly snorkel anywhere, MCWD identified five bays as eutrophic, meaning they are rich in nutrients that leads to algal blooms. These five bays may not offer the best snorkeling experience. They include: Stubbs Bay, Jennings Bay, West Arm, Halsted Bay, and Forest Lake.

Several of the A-grade bays are big water, such as Wayzata Bay and Spring Park Bay. The high traffic in these bays may make snorkeling difficult during the busy weekends. If you do go out, make sure your boat is securely anchored. And most importantly, stay close to your boat. You might also want to designate a watcher on board to alert you to any potential hazards.

***

Lake Minnetonka Shipwrecks

Lake Minnetonka remains a unique find in that it is the only lake in Minnesota that has been completely surveyed. Maritime Heritage Minnesota has identified 10 sites along with 152 anomalies.

- **Site 1**: *George/Excelsior* (1901-1909), 125-foot sternwheeler, burned as a public attraction

- **Site 2**: *Minneapolis* (1906-1912), 109-foot ferry, burned as a public attraction

- **Sites 3, 4, and 5**: *White Bear* (1906-1926), *Hopkins/Minnetonka* (1906-1949), *Como* (1906-1926), 70-foot streetcar boats, dismantled and sunk

- **Site 6**: *Hercules* (1917-1926), 50-foot steam tugboat, dismantled and sunk

- **Site 7**: The Wayzata Bay Wreck is a 85-foot wooden model barge that sunk during a storm on September 30, 1879. Model barges were an important part of American maritime history from 1860 through 1920, offering easier navigation and a strong, durable construction. The wreck is intact and the only site of its kind in the lake. It is only one of three extant examples of a boat of its kind in the entire country.

- **Site 8**: St. Albans Bay Wreck, possible dredge

- **Site 9**: Wreck 1, 50-foot structure possibly a launch or boat

- **Site 10**: Big Island pier

Note: Minnesota's submerged archaeological sites, including all wrecks and artifacts, are protected by state and federal laws, specifically, the Minnesota Field Archeology Act of 1983 and the federal, Abandoned Shipwreck Act of 1987. Sadly, all the known wrecks in Lake Minnetonka have been pillaged.

96

Beach Party!

As if you need an excuse! Lake Minnetonka has many beaches in all sizes from small neighborhood gems to larger public access sites like Excelsior Beach. Each one offers a different lake experience. Pack a lunch and find your place in the sun. Be sure to follow posted beach rules.

Note: Most parks do not permit alcohol. Beaches in Deephaven require a parking permit for up-close parking. Public parking is available farther from the beach.

Wayzata
Wayzata Beach
Information: 952-404-5300

Orono
Casco Beach
Between 2871 and 2879 Casco Point Road on Spring Park Bay
Information: 952-249-4600

Crescent Beach
240 Birch Bluff Road
Tonka Bay, MN
Information: 952-474-7994

Lydiard Beach
Lydiard Street on Carmans Bay
Information: 952-249-4600

Sandy Beach
At Cherry Avenue and Maple Place on North Arm Bay

Minnetonka Beach
Minnetonka Beach – Beach
Location: Cty Rd 15 W, 1/2 mile past the Arcola Bridge
Information: 952-939-8200

Mound
Surfside Park
Commerce Blvd
Information: 952-472-0600

Centerview Beach
On Centerview Lane
Information: 952-472-0600

Wychwood Beach
On Wilshire Boulevard
Information: 952-472-0600

Minnetrista
Lake Minnetonka Regional Park Beach
4610 County Road 44
Information: 763-694-7754

Shorewood/Tonka Bay
Crescent Beach
240 Birch Bluff Road
Tonka Bay, MN
Information: 952-474-7994

Wakota Beach
300 W. Point Road, Tonka Bay
Information: 952-474-7994

Excelsior
Excelsior Commons Beach
Corner of Lake and Water St..
Information: 952-474-5233

Deephaven
City of Deephaven 952-474-4755
Deephaven – Main Beach
19405 Lake Avenue

Sandy Beach
20300 Lakeview Avenue

Robinsons Bay Beach
3344 Robinsons Bay Road

Rocky Beach
20020 Lakeview Avenue.

Walden Beach
19355 Walden Trail

***

Snapshot of the 1960s

- 1960: The Sampson House in Excelsior closed

- 1960: Passenger train service to Excelsior ends

- 1964: The Gleason House in Wayzata was torn down

- 1964: The Rolling Stones performed live at the park's Danceland Pavilion to a crowd of about 300 fans

- 1965: F4 tornadoes rolled through the Lake Minnetonka area, killing thirteen people and injuring 175. It caused an estimated $51 million estimated damage and took out many local businesses at Jackson's Corner including the much-loved Maple Drive-In.

97

Ice It!

If you've ever seen the movie, *Grumpy Old Men*, you have a pretty good idea of what life is like on the lake during the winter. A great thing about Minnesotans is that we don't let winter chase us indoors. We just find new ways to enjoy it. That even applies to the lake. Sure, it's frozen over, but then how else will you get to ski across the ice or go ice fishing?

Just like back in the day, residents plowed roads on the ice. Going over the lake was the shortest route to a lot of places around the lake. The roads that appear on Spring Park Bay make it seem like nothing less than a city during ice fishing season.

The public dock at Excelsior is the entrance to the Lake Minnetonka dog park. Even the dogs like to get into the act. And there's no denying how fun it is to share a picture of yourself standing in the water next to the place that you docked earlier in the summer.

But don't be fooled. The snow on the ice can be just as deep or deeper than the snow on the land. You can't go wrong with a pair of cross country skis or snowshoes. But if you only seen a sheet of glass, remember the ice is slick no matter where you find it. The lake is certainly no exception. And be on the lookout for an ice yacht racing across the lake. When ideal conditions are available, it's time to hit the ice.

And the ice wasn't just for skating and skiing. In the days before refrigeration, the ice was harvested in blocks 14 to 24 inches thick for use in ice house storage and train transport. Every village around the lake had a storage facility.

Did You Know? In something that sounds like it needs a do-not-attempt warning, the winter sport of skijoring is when you are pulled by a horse, a dog, or car/truck on skis. Sounds like a Darwin Award contender, doesn't it? It comes from the Norwegian word meaning ski driving.

Safety first. Pay attention to those orange and white *Thin Ice* signs. They are placed there for a reason. As the Sheriff's Water Patrol reminds us every year, no ice is completely safe. It tends to be thinner under bridges and through channels. Also, some marinas and homeowners run aerators to keep the ice open to avoid damaging their docks.

Bonus Tip: Pay attention to where those ice houses are during the winter to get a heads-up on where to fish during the regular fishing season

Extra Bonus Tip: Remember those places that were best by water, but you couldn't see because you didn't have a boat? Well, now is the time to see the sights!

***

You Can Tell You're Not a Local When. . .

- You pronounce Wayzata as, well, how it's spelled rather than Why-zeta or Wise-zeta
- You've spent hours driving around the lake looking for that place from *Purple Rain* so you can get "*purified*"
- You wonder why it takes so long to get from Wayzata to Excelsior or vice versa
- You ask to see the martini menu at Haskell's
- You just have to take a selfie in front of the Port of Excelsior sign (Pssst! We've all done it.)

98

Take the Minnetonka Mills Walking Tour

While not in sight of Lake Minnetonka, Minnetonka Mills was vital to the early history of Lake Minnetonka. Founded in 1853, it was the hub of mill activity in the early days, hence, the name. If you look at Minnehaha Creek from the Burwell House, you can see the large swath that once formed the creek. That's because the creek was navigable by boat before the dam at Grays Bay was built. It was nothing like the creek you see today.

To learn about the village of Minnetonka Mills, follow the Minnetonka Mills Walking Tour. Figure on about an hour to leisurely follow the plan by sites that were important to the settlement of the area. The tour is best viewed with a tablet or laptop. It doesn't play nice with a smartphone. It contains a large archive of images. Make sure you have an adequate data plan to avoid extra charges. Your tour starts at the Burwell House.

13209 E. McGinty Road, Minnetonka
wjepson.com/mhstour/

***

Snapshot of the Modern Era

- 1971: Power Squadron acquires land on Big Island for a member retreat
- 1972: Frank Lloyd Wright's Little House was dismantled
- 1974: Excelsior Amusement Park closed down
- 1981: Discharged effulent from six of the seven wastewater treatment plants emptying into Lake Minnetonka are diverted
- 1986: Last wastewater treatment plant discharging effulent into Lake Minnetonka is diverted
- 1991: Tonka Toys moves out of Minnesota after its acquisition by Hasbro

99

Libbs Lake Beach Park

Connected to Lake Minnetonka via a channel, Libbs Lake Beach Park is located near Grays Bay. The park features picnicking, fishing, and swimming with public restrooms available. Parking is limited at this neighborhood beach.

Note: The park is closed for the 2016 due to road construction

16515 Park Lane, Minnetonka
Information: 952-939-8200
Hours: 8 a.m to 8 p.m. (Lifeguard on-site from noon to 6 p.m.)

***

You Know You're a Local When . . .

- You know where the restrooms are at Jake O'Connors

- You set up navigation on your phone to Wayzata just to hear the voice mispronounce the name. It never gets old

- You know how to navigate the lake in your boat even when the buoys are gone

- Snapper crossings, turtle crossings, and geese crossings are a way of life

- You know what a Blues Traveler is

- You know who Mister Jimmy was (Bonus points if you know his full name. Hint: Jimmy Hutmaker)

- You know the best walks in Excelsior are not just downtown

- You know *not* to try and get too close to the goslings—and so does your dog!

- You know how to exit the patio at Haskell's

- You have a pair of binoculars in your home and on your boat, or a spotting scope depending upon your means

100

Sail Away!

Sailing is as much a part of the Lake Minnetonka experience as any. And no matter what the weather, the boats are out. Half the fun is taking up the challenge of high winds and choppy water.

Lake Minnetonka's big waters provide the perfect setting to cross that learn-to-sail item off of your bucket list. Join a group session or set up private instruction. Go at your own pace with experienced instructors who will show you the ropes.

Would rather watch the action? Head on over to Wayzata. You can enjoy watching the Sunday afternoon regattas from Wayzata Beach, along the walk, or even from the docks at the Wayzata Depot.

Boating Classes
Lake Minnetonka Sailing School, Inc.
19802 Minnetonka Blvd., Deephaven
952-404-1645

Upper Minnetonka Yacht Club
Sailing instruction for children and adults
4165 Shoreline Drive, Spring Park
Information: 952-471-8783

***

Yacht Clubs on Lake Minnetonka

The Minnetonka Yacht Club (MYC) included members of the Breezy Point Club and The Highlands, two private men's clubs on Lake Minnetonka. Catboats or sloops that measured between 18 and 23 feet long were the vessels of choice. The first MYC regatta was held on August, 15, 1882. It began a tradition that still exists today.

But the MYC wasn't the only game in town. The Excelsior Yacht Club was established in 1883. It soon became clear that the lake wasn't big enough for both yacht clubs. By 1889, the two clubs merged into one. The clubhouse was built on Lighthouse Island in 1890. The club had 263 members and 62 boats over four classes.

Yet another yacht club got into the race. In 1965, the Wayzata Yacht Club (WYC) was established. Like the MYC, it too built a clubhouse in 1981. But if you think of yacht clubs are only about sailing, think again. In 1899, the Minnetonka Ice Yacht Club was formed on what was Tahtu Island.

The popularity of ice yachting exploded. From a mere five members at its launch, membership soared to 167 just two years later. Members ran several ice boats, ranging anywhere between 28 to 49 foot long. Imagine seeing that one racing across the ice! Some ice boats clocked speeds upward of 100 mph.

Alas, the ice yacht club was a short-term venture. In 1904, the clubhouse burned, never to be rebuilt. Like the Excelsior Yacht Club, it too merged with the MYC. Today, the hobby still lives on. When the ice is right, the ice boats are back on the lake, reliving this Lake Minnetonka tradition.

Other Events to Consider

Each community around the lake has its own share of local events, large and small. Here are a few of some other ones you may want to check out when looking for some fun things to do.

Excelsior
Burger and Bingo Fireworks Fundraiser (May)
10,000 Lakes Concours d'Elégance (June)
Annual Firefighter's Dance (July)
Lake Minnetonka BBQ and Beer Fest (August)
Holiday Tree Lighting (December)

Mound
Wheels 4 Meals Bike Ride (May)
Mound Fire Department Annual Fish Fry & Dance (June)
Taste of Tonka (September)
Christmas Tree Lighting Ceremony (November)
Tonka Brewfest (November)

Wayzata
Boo Blast (October)
Light Up the Lake Festival (Thanksgiving weekend)

A Final Word

What a journey! When we first moved to Lake Minnetonka in 2003, we had no idea how quickly we would fall in love with the lake. I hope it's the same for you.

Lake Minnetonka is big water, but also big in its draw. When we first boated here, we thought we floated into a dream. We did.

I hope you've enjoyed your adventures on Lake Minnetonka. Always remember that the lake is here to amuse you and to comfort you. It'll make you laugh and give you memories to last a life time. May you always remember the magic of its sparkling waters.

For Further Information

Wayzata Historical Society
wayzatahistoricalsociety.org

City of Wayzata
http://www.wayzata.org/

City of Orono
http://www.ci.orono.mn.us/

City of Minnetonka Beach
http://www.ci.minnetonka-beach.mn.us/

City of Spring Park
http://www.ci.spring-park.mn.us/

City of Mound
http://www.cityofmound.com/

Westonka Historical Society
http://westonkahistoricalsociety.org/index.html

City of Minnetrista
http://www.cityofminnetrista.com/

City of Shorewood
http://www.ci.shorewood.mn.us/

City of Tonka Bay
http://www.cityoftonkabay.net/

City of Excelsior
http://www.ci.excelsior.mn.us/

Excelsior Historical Society
https://www.elmhs.org/

City of Greenwood
http://www.greenwoodmn.com/

City of Deephaven
http://www.cityofdeephaven.org/

Deephaven Historical Society
http://deephavenhistorical.org/

City of Woodland
http://www.woodlandmn.org/

Works Cited

The 1893 Handbook and Souvenir of Lake Minnetonka. Lake Park Hotel, Lake Minnetonka, MN: Ellis & Gulick, 1893. Print.

"The Andrews Sisters – The Official Site." *The Andrews Sisters – The Official Site.*

"BoatUS Foundation – Online Courses." *BoatUS Foundation.*

"City of Orono, Minnesota ." *City of Orono*, Minnesota.

"City-Data.com." *City-Data.com.*

Dregni, Eric. *By the Waters of Minnetonka*. University of Minnesota Press: Minneapolis, MN, 2014. Print.

Dregni, Eric. "Prohibition on Lake Minnetonka." *Lake Minnetonka Magazine*, Mar. 2011. Web. 25 May 2016.

"Drowning Statistics." *Statistic Brain.*

Excelsior-Lake Minnetonka Historical Society.

"Fisheries Lake Surveys." : Minnesota DNR. <http://www.dnr.state.mn.us/lakefind/ showreport.html?downum=27013300>.

"Greater Wayzata Area Chamber of Commerce." *Wayzata History*.

Guide and Directory of Lake Minnetonka. Excelsior, MN: H.W. Mowry, 1884. Print.

Hammel, Bette Jones, and Karen Melvin. *Legendary Homes of Lake Minnetonka*. St. Paul, MN: Minnesota Historical Society, 2010. Print.

Hermit. Merriam-Webster. <http://www.merriam-webster.com/ dictionary/hermit>.

Holl, Jerry Wilson. *Picturesque Minnetonka: Commemorative Issue 1976*. Excelsior, MN: Excelsior-Lake Minnetonka Historical Society, 1976. Print.

Holst, Joanie, Lisa Stevens, and Elizabeth A. Vandam. *Images of America: Lake Minnetonka*. Arcadia Publishing: Charleston, South Carolina, 2015. Print.

Hornick, Jan, ed. *The Lake, The Land, and the People: A Historical Portrait of the City of Excelsior*. Excelsior, MN: City Council of the City of Excelsior, 1978. Print.

"The Inflation Calculator." *The Inflation Calculator*.

"James J. Hill." *Bio.com*. A&E Networks Television,.

"James J. Hill Lake Minnetonka History." *Lake Minnetonka Magazine*. Web.

Johnson, Frederick L., Thomas U. Tuttle, and Don Shelby. *The Big Water: Lake Minnetonka and Its Place in Minnesota History*. Minnetonka, MN: Deep Haven, 2012. Print.

Jones, Thelma. *Once upon a Lake: A History of Lake Minnetonka and Its People*. Minneapolis, MN: Ross and Haines, 1957. Print.

Koutsky, Kathryn Strand, and Linda Koutsky. *Minnesota Vacation Days: An Illustrated History*. St. Paul: Minnesota Historical Society, 2006. Print.

"Lafayette Club." *Lafayette Club.*

"MCWD: Minnehaha Creek Watershed District." MCWD: Minnehaha Creek Watershed District. <http://minnehahacreek.org/>.

Merriman, Ann and Christopher Olson. *Lake Minnetonka Survey 1 Report*. Maritime Heritage Minnesota, 2012.

Meyer, Ellen Wilson. *Picturesque Deephaven*. Excelsior, MN: Excelsior-Lake Minnetonka Historical Society, 1989. Print.

Meyer, Ellen Wilson. *Happenings around Deephaven: The First Hundred Years, 1853-1953*. Excelsior, MN: Excelsior-Lake Minnetonka Historical Society, 1978. Print.

Meyer, Ellen Wilson. *Lake Minnetonka's Historic Hotels*. Excelsior, MN: Excelsior-Lake Minnetonka Historical Society, 1997. Print.

Meyer, Ellen Wilson., and Jerry Wilson. Holl. *Happenings around Wayzata: The First Hundred Years, 1853-1953*. Excelsior, MN: Tonka Print., 1980. Print.

"Minnesota Highway History Primer: 1917-1934." Minnesota Highway History Primer. <http://deadpioneer.com/articles/primer.htm>.

MnDOT History." Minnesota Department of Transportation. <http://www.dot.state.mn.us/information/history.html>.

Ogland, James W. *Lake Minnetonka Insights: Discovery and Legends.* Wayzata, MN: Dnalgo Publications, 2010. Print.

Ogland, James W. *Picturing Lake Minnetonka: A Postcard History.* St. Paul, MN: Minnesota Historical Society, 2001. Print.

Peterson, Roger Tory. *A Field Guide to Birds: Giving Field Marks of All Species Found East of the Rockies.* 4th ed. Boston: Houghton Mifflin, 1980. Print.

"Public Boating Courses." Tonka Channels. <http://www.minnetonkaps.org/weblog/?page_id=201>.

Richards, Bergmann. *Early Background of Minnetonka Beach.* Minnetonka Beach, MN: Minnetonka Beach Long Range Planning Committee, 1957. Print.

Rockvam, Tom. *Growing up on Lake Minnetonka.* Vol. 4. Mound, MN: T. Rockvam, 2010. Print.

"St. Martin's By-the-Lake Episcopal Church." *St. Martin's By-the-Lake Episcopal Church.*

Storm Prediction Center – NOAA. "Beaufort Wind Scale." Beaufort Wind Scale. Storm Prediction Center – NOAA, n.d. Web. 01 Apr. 2016.

Tester, John R., and Mary Keirstead. *Minnesota's Natural Heritage: An Ecological Perspective.* Minneapolis: U of Minnesota, 1995. Print.

Walking the Trails of History: A Tour Guide to Historic Places in Excelsior, Minnesota. Excelsior, MN: Excelsior-Lake Minnetonka Historical Society, 2002. Print.

"Wayzata Historical Society." *Wayzata Historical Society.*

"Welcome to Your One-stop Resource for Everything Fishing and Boating." *Take Me Fishing.*

Wilson, Blanche Nichols. *Minnetonka Story; a Series of Stories Covering Lake Minnetonka's Years from Canoe to Cruiser.* Minneapolis: Colwell, 1950. Print.

Wilson Meyer, Ellen. *Happenings Around Deephaven.* Excelsior, MN: Excelsior-Lake Minnetonka Historical Society, 1978. Print.

Wilson Meyer, Ellen. *Tales from Tonka.* Excelsior, MN: Excelsior-Lake Minnetonka Historical Society, 1993. Print.

Wolfe, Joan, Mary Stacke, Rich Sladek, and Mike Revier. *Navarre: The Hub of Lake Minnetonka: A Guide to History and the Community.* Orono, MN: Navarre Community Initiative, 2014. Print.

About the Author

Chris Dinesen Rogers was born in the suburban Chicago area. Acting on her love for the outdoors and conservation, she volunteered with Brookfield Zoo and the Illinois Department of Natural Resources.

Chris has worked with the US Forest Service, US Fish and Wildlife Service, and the Nature Conservancy. She and her husband, Norm, continued volunteering for environmental causes with the National Park Service at Mammoth Cave National Park in Kentucky. In 2000, Chris and Norm were awarded the state of Kentucky Colonel honor for their work in restoring parts of Mammoth Cave.

In 2002, Chris began her own art business, Weborg Lodge Studio. Creativity continues to be a driving force with her. Chris is now a freelance writer, promoting conservation and health education.

Other Books by the Author

Non-Fiction:

101 Things to Do on the Wisconsin Great River Road
All Plants Are Edible Once
101 Tips for the Adventurous Cook
How to Achieve Your Fitness and Wellness Potential

Fiction:

Murder to Order

Available on Amazon, CreateSpace, and Your Favorite Bookseller

Made in the USA
Lexington, KY
19 August 2018